YoungWriters 2005 POETR

PLAYGROUN

Let your creativity flow...

ode
limerick   haiku
rhyme
balla

- Inspirations From
Devon & Cornwall
Edited by Donna Samworth

 Young**Writers**

First published in Great Britain in 2006 by:
Young Writers
Remus House
Coltsfoot Drive
Peterborough
PE2 9JX
Telephone: 01733 890066
Website: www.youngwriters.co.uk

SB ISBN 1 84602 353 X

Foreword

Young Writers was established in 1991 and has been passionately devoted to the promotion of reading and writing in children and young adults ever since. The quest continues today. Young Writers remains as committed to the fostering of burgeoning poetic and literary talent as ever.

This year's Young Writers competition has proven as vibrant and dynamic as ever and we are delighted to present a showcase of the best poetry from across the UK. Each poem has been carefully selected from a wealth of *Playground Poets* entries before ultimately being published in this, our thirteenth primary school poetry series.

Once again, we have been supremely impressed by the overall high quality of the entries we have received. The imagination, energy and creativity which has gone into each young writer's entry made choosing the best poems a challenging and often difficult but ultimately hugely rewarding task - the general high standard of the work submitted amply vindicating this opportunity to bring their poetry to a larger appreciative audience.

We sincerely hope you are pleased with our final selection and that you will enjoy *Playground Poets - Inspirations From Devon & Cornwall* for many years to come.

Contents

Cubert School, Newquay

Ellacombe Primary School, Torquay

Fremington Community Primary & Nursery School, Barnstaple

Sam Tithecott (9)   62
Thomas Hyam (9)   63

Heamoor CP School, Penzance
Matthew Bone (10)   63
Luke Jenkin (10)   64
Scarlett Cohen (9)   64
Ben Hardy (9)   65
Louisa Bonner (10)   65
Robert Dunn (11)   66
Shannen Louise Stringer (10)   66
Oliver Jack Marston (9)   67
Grace Carter (10)   67
Adam Prowse & George Jackson (10)   68
Jasmine Rayner (10) & Jamie-Leigh Lobb   68
Drew Maguire (10)   69
Chloe Carley & Kerryanne Taylor (10)   69
Beth Marshall (9)   70
Jordan Johnstone (9)   70
Rhys Brownfield (11) & Oliver Angove (10)   71
Marcel Torode (10)   71
Daisy Jenkins (10)   72
Hannah Griffith (10)   72
Breon Day-Nicholls (9)   73
Stefan Osborne & George Mitchell (10)   73
Lauren Date (9)   74
Lauren Ridge (10)   74
Ryan Hosken (9)   75
Izzy Williams (10)   75
Olaf Marshall Whitley (9)   76
Rebecca Ingram (10)   76
Kerenza Mitchell (9)   77
Merrion Steer (9)   78
Harry Eden Trezona (9)   79
Shannon Moseley (9)   80
Jasmine Hannah Huckle (9)   81
Steven Platts (9)   81
Billy Read (9)   82
Jack James (9)   82
Matthew Quick & Jamie Dennis (10)   83

Lady Seaward's School, Exeter

Ella MacPhee (10)	84
Codie Wilson (9)	84
Shane Thomas Dougan (11)	84
Oliver Cassidy-Butler (10)	85
Alice Elizabeth Johnson (10)	85
Jamie May (11)	86

Manor Primary School, Ivybridge

Kirsty Sutton (8)	87
Freddie Monk & Ellie Smith (7)	87
George Turns (7)	88
Charlotte Stemp (8)	88
Jasmin Bird (8)	89
Kai Whelbourne (8)	89
Charlie Tapp (8)	90
Nicole Grech-Cini (8)	90
Ella Beardsley (7)	90
Hayley Dennis (8)	91
Kyah-Nicole Evans (8)	91
James Stirk (8)	91
Cara Alcock (7)	92
Freya Taylor (7)	92
Nathanael Marklew (8)	93
Connor Chilcott & Jacob Horgan (8)	93
Jacob Antony Meads (8)	93
Michael Beddard (7)	94
Benjamin Timothy Douglass (8)	94
Hollie Manlow (8)	95
Jay Gloyn (8)	95
Amy Flower (8)	95
Barnaby Shaw (8)	96
Phoebe Phillips (7)	96
Oliver Brandon (7)	96
Amy Gibson (9)	97
Scott Ham (9)	97
James Scott Ogle (8)	98
Amber Bartlett (8)	98
Chloe Ellen Fancett (7)	98
Karina Jones (7)	99
Alice May Handley (8)	99

Blake Alexander Chapman (8)   99
Nathan Faulkner (8)   100
Tristan Read (7)   100
Brendan James Rosier (7)   100
Kieran J Brown (7)   101
Matt Buckley (8)   101
Chloë Williams (8)   101

St Joseph's Catholic Primary School, Devonport
Jonathon Pink (8)   102
Liam Ferguson (10)   102
Rebecca Pink (9)   103
Cohen Officer (8)   103
Lauren Winchester (8)   104
Emily Futcher (9)   104
Maeve Dennehy (9)   105
Lucy Fowell (7)   106

Stowford Primary School, Ivybridge
Matthew Luke (11)   106
Keziah Stephenson (10)   107

Stuart Road Primary School, Stoke
Jordan Kane (8)   108
Sunni Elder (7)   108
Eleanor Aquitaine (7)   108
Miluse Hokyova & Ashley Russell (7)   109
Megan Rowland (7)   109
Harry Hayward (8)   109
Eleanor Cheesman (7)   110
Ritchie Reynolds (7)   110
Josh Snow (7)   110
Lewis Withers (7)   111
Danielle Hines (8)   111
Taylor Olver (8)   111
Kathryn Wardle (8)   112
Tobias Moore (7)   112
Rebecca Welbourn (8)   112
Josana Hayles (8)   113
Shannon Nation (8)   113

Olivia Evenden (8)	114
Vasily Babichev (8)	114
Dylan George (8)	115
Oliver Newton (8)	115
Daniel Collier (8)	115
Carmen Kirkby (8)	116
George May (8)	116
Teddy Thompson (8)	117
Lauren Stewart (8)	117
Nathan Kerr (7)	117
Jack Robinson (8)	118
Thomas Bellamy (8)	118
Kiera Symons (8)	118
Aimee Boniface (8)	119
Jack Pullinger-Ham (8)	119
Hannah Sansom (8)	119
Millie Brown (8)	120
Chantel Jenkins (8)	120
Ellie Jackson (9)	121
Hannah Atkins (8)	121
Adam Olver (8)	122

Tidcombe Primary School, Tiverton

Amy Marshall (10)	122
Caragh Matthews (10)	123
Louise Dunn (10)	123
Dominic Mottram (10)	124
Madeleine Ell (10)	124
Megan Pharaoh (10)	125
Joseph Taylor (10)	126
Amber Gannon (11)	127
Lauren Pincombe (11)	128
Dylan Penberthy (10)	129
Bethany Morrish (10)	130
Robbie Pengelly (11)	130
Sarah Taylor (10)	131
Yasmin Huish (10)	131
Elliott Howells (10)	132
Josie Russell-Cox (10)	132
Eloise Harcombe (11)	133
Grace Drew (10)	133

Nathanael Kidner (10)   134
Gemma Mogford (10)   134
Katie Stribley (10)   135
Crystal Gardiner (10)   135

Tregadillett Community Primary School, Launceston
Hannah Stagg (8)   136
Daniel Pike (8)   137
Joanna Turvill (9)   138
Hugh Harvey (8)   138
Nathan James (8)   139
Lucy Hamilton (8)   139
Evie Tummon (8)   140

Tregony Primary School, Truro
Lucy Grayston (7)   140
Georgina Green (8)   141
Benjamin Humphries (7)   141
Katie Cadby (9)   142
Michael Berridge (9)   142
Eleanor Gulliford (7)   142
Bethany Grant (8)   143
Jasper Boden (7)   143
Harry Price (8)   143
Rose Dixon (7)   144
Kai Pearce (8)   144
Jasmine McMorran (9)   144
Sophie Jackson (9)   145
Joshua Griffiths (8)   145
Jack Emery (9)   145
Andrew Barnes (9)   146
Jamie Lee (9)   146
Rachael O'Brien (9)   146
Ysabelle Smith (8)   147

Troon Primary School, Camborne
Noal Fawdry (10)   147
Mylor Fawdry (10)   148
Jake Bowles (9)   148
Charlotte Wardley (10)   149

Andrew Figgins (10)	149
Amy Dillow (10)	150
Tamara Browning (10)	150
Curtis Wherry (9)	151
Jacob Rail (10)	151
Amy Greig (9)	152
Liam Stone (10)	152
James Wassell (9)	153
Elena Hoskin (10)	153
Aaron Roskilly (9)	154
Josh Trescowthick (10)	154

Woodbury CE Primary School, Exeter

Mark Godfrey (9)	155
Josephine Jacka	155
Heidi Thiemann (10)	156
Ollie Woodley	156
James Ubank (10)	157
George Drew (10)	157
Grace Ratley (10)	158
Katie Hester (10)	158
Megan Pewsey	159
Barnaby Lovell	160
Josh Levontine (10)	161
Jozie Bannister (10)	162
Poppy Joyce (8)	163
Jocelyn Mennell (10)	164

The Poems

I'm A Fox

Feet thump!
Stomp, stomp!
Children running all around
Hear their footstep on the ground.
Hedgehogs sneaking.
Robins peeking.
What a sight to see
A child's looking straight at me.
I scuttled down my den,
What if there were men
Wandering around with guns?
That would not be fun.
I scampered out of my den.
The woodlands were empty once again.

Amy Hunter (10)
Bickleigh-on-Exe Primary School, Tiverton

A Birthday Poem

Birthdays are exciting
Birthdays are just madness
Birthdays are the only day
When your brain is filled with gladness!

It's nearly my own birthday
I'm rolling about in bed
This year I've been very naughty
My mum and dad have said.

I've just woken up from bed
And there's something that I've found
My parents are very generous
They've given me less than a pound!

Marnik Loysen (10)
Bickleigh-on-Exe Primary School, Tiverton

Abbie

Cream in colour with bright brown eyes
That look so innocent when mischievous and playful.
Her coat so soft it feels like a bundle of silk.
She runs around in circles chasing her big fluffy tail.
She looks so funny when she topples back in a heap on the floor
And her legs in the air.
Her wet, black nose means she's healthy and well.
She's more than a puppy, she's really good company.
Abbie really is Man's best friend.

Tess Burgess (10)
Bickleigh-on-Exe Primary School, Tiverton

Rice!

I was walking with my family one day
When I spotted my friends on the way.
They were walking their pets talking about their holiday.
I said, 'No way, I would rather stay with my family.'
That had caught their swimming eyes.
They stood there in surprise.
They started talking about some sort of rice.
I presumed it tasted nice.

Keanna Maryan (10)
Bickleigh-on-Exe Primary School, Tiverton

My Poem About A Playground

Big kids running and shuffling to get to the shed.
They get all grumpy if they don't get a hockey stick.

The little kids queuing for the bouncy hoppers.
The other kids walking and sucking their lollies and never stop.

They're puffing and purring like a dog and cat.

Shannon Wiggins (9)
Bickleigh-on-Exe Primary School, Tiverton

This Man

This man with a loud voice.
This man with crazy hair.
This man with eyes that glare.
This man in a colourful jacket.
This man carrying a packet.
This man is ready, this man is poised
As he walks into the stands to support his team
And shouts, 'Come on, boys.'

Josh Bradshaw (10)
Bickleigh-on-Exe Primary School, Tiverton

Train Set - Haikus

My Hornby train set
I enjoy playing with it
It gives hours of fun.

Hornby and Bachman
Are two makes of model trains
I have got both these.

Tom Huxtable (11)
Bickleigh-on-Exe Primary School, Tiverton

Who Am I?

I'm hiding in the bushes waiting to strike
On my unsuspecting victim in the dark of the night.

As the stage coach rounds the bend,
I shout, 'Your money or your life will end.'

They gave me their money, I melted back into the night
And waited for the next victim, to give them a *fright!*

Tanith Wyatt Gould (10)
Bickleigh-on-Exe Primary School, Tiverton

One Night

It's a dark and creepy night
Wind gusting
Sounds of the wolves howling
I hear the kitchen door creak
I lay still in bed like a sleeping lion
I hear mysterious footsteps
I grab my torch
I tiptoe to my bedroom door like a ballerina
I open the door, no one is there
I creep down the stairs
I reach the ancient kitchen door
I count to three then open the door
It creaks like the sound of a baby shrieking
To my surprise no one is there
I look behind the door
Then look outside
Still there is no one there
I take a few steps towards the door
Open the cupboard door
All I see are pink wellington boots
I go back to my bedroom
I am still listening
I eventually fall asleep
I wake the next morning and think,
Was that real or just a dream?

Alex Dudley (10)
Bickleigh-on-Exe Primary School, Tiverton

My Tractor - Haiku

My tractor is fun
Travelling on my farmland
I am so lucky.

Tom Palmer (10)
Bickleigh-on-Exe Primary School, Tiverton

Red Arrows

Zigging, zagging way up high
Painting pictures in the sky
Dancing, prancing, flying all around
I hope I don't hit the ground
Streaking blue, flashing red
Pretty soon I could be dead.
Zipping, zapping, flying all around
Gosh! Nearly hit the ground
Zipping past in a flash
Sorry, folks, I've got to dash
The show is over
Now I'm done
I'm going off to have some *fun!*

Marshall Bernhardt (11)
Bickleigh-on-Exe Primary School, Tiverton

My Family

I am part of a family
Mum and Dad
Brothers who are older and drive me mad
Cousins and aunties
Uncles a few
Granny and Grandpa
Grandad too
Then there is Grandma
Generous and kind
Ready for action
With a great mind.

Emily Shaw (10)
Bickleigh-on-Exe Primary School, Tiverton

Scrumpy

I have a pet called Scrumpy
Who's very, very grumpy.
He scratches and bites whoever is nice,
Who comes in the den of his.
He sleeps all day and night
And gives me terrible frights.
He runs and fights
And catches prey at night.
So don't mess with Scrumpy.
He greets me at the door
Licking his great big paw.
Looks tired and weary,
Scary and sleepy.
Could I love him even more?

George Chamberlin (9)
Bickleigh-on-Exe Primary School, Tiverton

My Dog Kennings

Bone chewer
Tail wagger
Squirrel chaser
Cat hater
Frisbee catcher
Walk lover
Firework fearer
Non obeyer
Good sniffer
My dog Josh.

Ben Colston (10)
Bickleigh-on-Exe Primary School, Tiverton

Family

Dad tall,
Mum small.
Brothers are a pain,
Baby's bottom's always smelling.
Afraid to invite friends around for tea.
Toys scattered,
Shoes everywhere.
Pushchairs and prams in the way.
Baby getting annoying once again.
Dogs barking, can't hear the music on the TV.
Go outside to get away.
Mum and Dad come looking.
Rain starts to fall,
Go back in.
Baby stops crying.
Go in your room,
Brother comes in and shouts at you.

Emmé-Lou Mitchell (10)
Bickleigh-on-Exe Primary School, Tiverton

My Furry Friends

I have two cats
One is called Sweepy
And the other is called Tiger.
Sweepy is black and white like a panda.
She is fluffy like a teddy bear.
Her eyes are round and bright like the sun.
Tiger has teeth like a sharp razor.
He's got eyes like a snake and he is fluffy like a rabbit.
They are my two best friends.

Ellis Budd (10)
Bickleigh-on-Exe Primary School, Tiverton

A Poem About Seasons

In springtime it is peaceful
Because the blossom comes out
And the lambs start bouncing about.
Then it's summer when the sun gets hotter
So we go outside and play.
Some go in the swimming pool or stay indoors all day.
Then it's autumn, the days are shorter and colder
And the leaves start falling like rain falling down from the sky
And harvest is coming again.
Now winter is here
It's cold, snowing and the wind is blowing
And the trees are bare
But I don't care
Because Christmas is near.
My favourite time of the year.

Jake Dascombe (10)
Bickleigh-on-Exe Primary School, Tiverton

Firework Night

Bang! The fireworks burst.
Boom! The colours glisten.
Blast! The light shimmers.
Bang, boom, blast!
It echoes like thunder, gunpowder - *boom!*

Crash! The fire lapping.
Clang! It's spitting.
Crash, clang, boom!

Charlotte Alsopp (10)
Bickleigh-on-Exe Primary School, Tiverton

My Guinea Pigs

So cute, so fluffy,
They're like a pillow,
Faces that make you go *argh*.
Their squeaking always gets your attention,
Being hungry all the time,
Waddling and tapping as they move across the ground.

Munching, crunching and chewing the food,
Nice to see them every day
Just staring at you for more food
Like they haven't been fed for ages.
Hopping around when they're happy and excited,
Giggling and purring to be loved more.
They're lovely to hug and cuddle
And someone to talk to who will listen,
Well, hopefully.

Katie Harwood (10)
Bickleigh-on-Exe Primary School, Tiverton

Croatia's Colours

The white sails swaying in the cool breeze,
The blue sea shimmering in the midday sun.
The red water glowing as the sun sets,
The pink tiled roofs sitting side by side.
The green pine trees standing tall like soldiers,
The silver fish gliding through the water like a dart.

White, blue, red, pink, green and silver
Are the colours of my holiday.

Jack Richardson (10)
Bickleigh-on-Exe Primary School, Tiverton

The Hunt

The grass moves from side to side
   As the people sleep,
A giant is stalking.
   The wind is blowing,
An attack is imminent.
   On one side is the hunter,
On the other side the hunted.
   The lightning flashes,
It's going to start.
   On one side is the chaser,
On the other the runner.
   It pounces and bites!
Then there's a struggle,
   A shout of pain
And when the silence of death takes its toll.
   The cat has its reward.

Mark English (10)
Bickleigh-on-Exe Primary School, Tiverton

Lions

Lions are my favourite animals
I love their yellow coats
Their manes are soft and fluffy
Their roar is loud and clear

Lionesses do the hunting
Watch out zebra and antelope
The cubs have spots and are playful

They live in Africa
In groups called prides
They sit by day in the shade
They have no enemies
And are known as the 'King of Beasts'.

Kathryn Letheren (11)
Bickleigh-on-Exe Primary School, Tiverton

Kraken

A huge, mythical monster,
A tyrannical terror,
A world threat.
The deadly beast sleepeth on the murky seabed
Until a ship unknowingly sails into the sea monster's territory.
The ship lands on an island unlike any other
And then the Kraken has his feast.

Jamie Freed (10)
Bickleigh-on-Exe Primary School, Tiverton

You And Me

If I am fun you are boring.
If I am good you are bad.
If I am fast you are slow.
If I am young you are old.
If I am me you are you.
If I am dead you are alive.

Zac Smith (10)
Bickleigh-on-Exe Primary School, Tiverton

Joining In
(Inspired by 'Left Out' by Celia Warren)

I feel as happy as a clown on a unicycle.
I feel like a kangaroo jumping on a trampoline.
I feel like a dog getting his belly rubbed.
I feel like I've just been laughed at
By a smile that looks like a banana.

Jack Hamlyn (9)
Clyst Honiton CE Primary School, Exeter

My Shop

(Inspired by 'My Grandmother' by Elizabeth Jennings)

It has taken hold
I'm much too old
To look after my shop
My shop, my shop
My shop.

It's like I'm glued
I can't bear to go out to buy food
All because of my shop
My shop, my shop
My shop.

I like the smell
Of where I dwell
Which is in my shop
My shop, my shop
My shop.

I love the Apostle spoons
And the book that says about moons
Which all live in my shop
My shop, my shop
My shop.

Harry Palmer (9)
Clyst Honiton CE Primary School, Exeter

Grandmother's Antique Shop

(Inspired by 'My Grandmother' by Elizabeth Jennings)

I own an antique shop,
With big things,
And small things.
I own an antique shop.

I own an antique shop,
With long things,
And short things.
I own an antique shop.

Holly Bedford (9)
Clyst Honiton CE Primary School, Exeter

Grandmother's Shop

(Inspired by 'My Grandmother' by Elizabeth Jennings)

I've got pots and pans
And various cans
I've got china plates
And lots of crates

I've got polish
To demolish
The dust on my antiques
To keep them so shiny

I've got clocks
I've got rocks
I've got socks
I've got cupboards and sideboards as well

The customers come in
To get my antiques
It would take less than a week
It makes me feel happy

I've got china in stacks
And lots of racks
But I feel good
Because of the wood

I get money and money
And queues and queues
I love my shop
And I feel that it loves me.

Kieran Lewis (10)
Clyst Honiton CE Primary School, Exeter

Grandmother's Shop

(Inspired by 'My Grandmother' by Elizabeth Jennings)

Grandmother has a shop on the end of the street
She has a lovely perfume but has stinky feet.

She has a collection of spoons
And a sack of bowls,
I think she thinks the planet
Has two moons,
She's got an old picture of two moles.

She has a grandfather clock,
In the window of her shop.
Sometimes I go there for tea,
Then she gets in a muddle
And I give her a cuddle.

Amber Bedford (9)
Clyst Honiton CE Primary School, Exeter

My Journey

It was so quiet that I heard
The sweet, little birds sing.
It was so calm that I heard
A spider spin its silky web.
It was so silent that I could feel and hear
The crunch and the crackle of the autumn leaves.
It was so peaceful that I heard
The church bells ding and dong
As they called the people from the street.
It was so serene that I heard
A drop and a trickle of the crystal-clear stream.
It was so still that I heard
A breeze of wind come gently
Through the soft, winding willow trail.

Elanor Cutcliffe (7)
Collaton St Mary CE (VA) Primary School, Paignton

Autumn

The
Leaves
Are dark
Chocolate
And crispy crisps
Swaying in the wind
The trees are bare, plucked
Chickens standing tall and straight
The streets are cold and lonely like a
Grave, the ground is covered in leaves
Which make a warm, cosy
Blanket, the seas are lonely
And cold like a still, dead flower
In your garden. Autumn is
Finally here, soon winter
Will strike and you will
See no beauty.

Rebecca Thom (9)
Collaton St Mary CE (VA) Primary School, Paignton

Autumn

The trees are tall
The trees are slim
The grass is green
Its blades are thin
Chocolate-brown
Cherry-red and sunshine-yellow
Whirling, whirling, whirling around
Slowly carpeting the ground
The leaves crunch beneath my feet
Crunch, crunch, crunch
When the last leaf falls
Everyone knows autumn time
Has just begun.

Krystal King (10)
Collaton St Mary CE (VA) Primary School, Paignton

My Journey Around The School

It was so serene that I heard
The dead leaves crunch beneath
My feet.
It was so quiet that I heard
A buzzing bee collecting pollen for
Its family.
It was so restful that I saw
The old stone church standing alone
Surrounded by trees.
It was so calm that I saw
The willow winding like an
Ancient forest.
It was so tranquil that I heard
A spider spin its silky web.
It was so still that I heard
The cold breeze sweep through
My hair.

Bethany Stevens (7)
Collaton St Mary CE (VA) Primary School, Paignton

Autumn

The
Leaves are
Brown chocolate
Melting on a long hot day.
The trees are big chunky elephants
Sitting down on a summer's night.
The moon is a bright new pin
Gazing onto the ground
Below.
The king and queen will bow in
Their time and autumn will come
Again.

Kristina Topic (9)
Collaton St Mary CE (VA) Primary School, Paignton

Autumn

The leaves' fall is a
Graceful eagle in flight,
The feathery leaves are playful
Children, with a pile of crisp, autumn
Leaves in front of them,
The golden heart of the forest is owed to autumn,
The autumn colour is the warm, first smile of a baby,
The sturdy forest is a wall of bare bodies,
The hard-earned leaves are wrinkly smiles,
The bark is milk chocolate melting in golden swarms of leaves.

A
U
T
U
M
N.

Victoria Blanchard (9)
Collaton St Mary CE (VA) Primary School, Paignton

Autumn

The leaves
are brown chocolate,
falling from outstretched
fingers. The calm, mystical king
of autumn has taken the beloved crown from
the summer king. The birds are missiles darting
into the water. The silent wind is blowing the
canopy of leaves back and forth, never stopping,
always blowing. The autumn sun shows the
wrinkled faces of the ancient trees. Many tales
they have to tell, many things they have seen.

Adam Bennett (9)
Collaton St Mary CE (VA) Primary School, Paignton

Summer

Summer, a pheasant
Of emerald
Sitting on her
Golden throne

Summer, an amber bird
Tweeting her harmony
To the bronze
Oak trees

Summer, a glowing hawk
Gliding upon
The forest
Searching for her prey

Summer, a dove
Swooping through the
Crystal pool of blue
Setting the marshmallow
Clouds upon the silver horizon.

Kimberley Illman (10)
Collaton St Mary CE (VA) Primary School, Paignton

Storm

Storm, a ferocious, ghostly planet,
Darkness surrounds.
Smashing sea destroys everything
In its path,
Darkness, the jaws of death.
Storm, destroyer of all.
Rocks shattered,
Trees demolished.
Leaves tossing and turning
Trying to escape from the
Horrific wind.
Storm is a ferocious, ghostly planet.

Joshua Vidler (10)
Collaton St Mary CE (VA) Primary School, Paignton

Autumn

The crown prince of autumn
Of crispy, crunchy leaves.
His sword
A blade twinkling and slicing
At the russet, golden trees
Making them
Bone-bare.

His armour glistening
Like the autumn sun
Through the trees,
Sunlight rays strike his armour
Slicing the last tree of autumn.

The prince is dying,
He needs a tree to live.
He searches high in the hills
But there is nothing
Only the tree of autumn -
It cannot be touched by a soul
Only the crown prince of autumn.

Dominic Lloyd (10)
Collaton St Mary CE (VA) Primary School, Paignton

Autumn

The autumn turns the grass into a sea of gold soldiers
The bare branches are the arms of an octopus
In the crispy leaf sea
The chocolate nut leaves crunch under your feet
As the bald heads of trees wrinkle in the hot weather
The trees are bold statues made of crispy leaves
And the chocolate bark melts
In the yellow rose sun.

Naomi Yarrell (9)
Collaton St Mary CE (VA) Primary School, Paignton

Fog

Fog has a hidden secret
    Very quiet,
        Very still.
Fog, a ghostly ship,
    Very calm,
        Very helpful.
His life envelopes our world,
    So kind,
        So beautiful.
Embracing you with such tenderness,
    Loving you with such care.

His misty body will never fade away
    Away,
        Away.
His delicate fingers shine pleasantly,
    Warmly,
Against the black, night sky,
Sprinkled with a myriad glistening stars.
He leaves.

Kirby Court (10)
Collaton St Mary CE (VA) Primary School, Paignton

My Journey Around The School

It was so peaceful that I heard
The soft, flowing water rush down the river
It was so quiet that I heard
Rushing and crunching of the leaves
It was so still that I heard
The car rushing from side to side
It was so cold that I heard
The wind ripple through my hair
It was so silent that I heard
The song of the church.

Oliver Nixon (7)
Collaton St Mary CE (VA) Primary School, Paignton

Autumn - Cinquain

Autumn
Autumn is near
Leaves are falling in fright
Squirrels are scuttling on trees
Look, look.

Eleanor Bonstow (9)
Collaton St Mary CE (VA) Primary School, Paignton

Autumn - Cinquain

Autumn
Bronze leaves falling
Crimson, crispy carpets
Bruising leaves and twigs in the cold
Dying . . .

Christopher Kelly (8)
Collaton St Mary CE (VA) Primary School, Paignton

Autumn

Sparkling silver webs
Orange leaves raising proud
Squirrels climbing up oak trees
Listen . . .

Grace Davies (8)
Collaton St Mary CE (VA) Primary School, Paignton

Autumn - Cinquain

Listen
Autumn's whirling,
You note the tumbling leaves,
Watch the snapping twigs fly past you,
Sssshhhhhh, sssshhhhhh.

Harriet Hern (8)
Collaton St Mary CE (VA) Primary School, Paignton

Fog

The ghost ship of nowhere
Appears in front of my eyes.
Fog, treacherous and vile.

Ship has disappeared,
A sheet of ghostly mist
Whirling,
Twirling
Around and around,
Haunting this land.

World suffocated
By shrouds of
Fog, fog, fog
Everywhere,
Ship gone,
Sight gone,
I am all alone.

Gabrielle Thom (11)
Collaton St Mary CE (VA) Primary School, Paignton

Autumn

Autumn
Meanders in and out
The golden trees
Taking his place from
Summer.

All the green leaves have
Vanished.

Turned golden and falling on
To the soft, autumn ground.

The sound of crunching
Leaves whisper and sob
As they tumble from the treetops.

Sarah Stacey (10)
Collaton St Mary CE (VA) Primary School, Paignton

Autumn

Autumn, the queen of hues
Her face glows a burnished amber
Waving her iridescent cloak
Over the saffron sky
Setting trees and plants to rest

She strides aback of her chestnut mare
Cantering through the lush, green wood
Transforming its colour into
Gold,
Crimson.
Ginger.

Her presence brings joy and peace
How kind, loving, caring
A person with a magnificent name
Flourishing autumn glade.

Kristian Stapleton (11)
Collaton St Mary CE (VA) Primary School, Paignton

Storm

Storm grasps sailors to the heart of the sea
Dragging them
Down
Down
Down
To death where no one
Has gone before
Whipping the sea
Twisting and turning
Turning and twisting
Making a clear path
To petrify the seabed
Planting a tornado in its depths.

Ashley Fenton (10)
Collaton St Mary CE (VA) Primary School, Paignton

Autumn

Autumn
A beautiful bronze princess
Dressed in emerald-gold
Dancing in the wonderful summer
Breeze

Drifting
Through the glinting waterfall
She paints an autumn picture
With crimson
Amber
And saffron colours

Leaves tumble to the ground
In a ruby cascade
Trees whisper for autumn has come
Best clothing of scarlet
Colours will be worn
For the autumn ball tonight
Autumn
Is here.

Rosina Morfey (10)
Collaton St Mary CE (VA) Primary School, Paignton

Fog

A frosty feeling
Glows its faintest glimmer
Draining your vision
Fog, like a ghostly image
Menacing spirits devour all minds
Spreading over an icy hand
Clinging beauty over firm mists
Murmuring mists leave a faint trace
Like a mysterious ghost
Floating through dreams of silky darkness.

Jamie Taylor (10)
Collaton St Mary CE (VA) Primary School, Paignton

Autumn - Cinquain

Autumn
In dignity
Battling, golden leaves
Wind hushing in the breeze gently
Tranquil . . .

Antony Brierley (8)
Collaton St Mary CE (VA) Primary School, Paignton

Autumn - Cinquain

Autumn
Leaves are falling
To the carpet so crisp
Red, orange, amber, bronze, beige too,
You watch!

Ayse Cetin (9)
Collaton St Mary CE (VA) Primary School, Paignton

Autumn - Cinquain

Autumn
Crunchy red leaves
Sparkling silver webs tear
Wind blowing through the forest trees
Winter.

Daniel Bamford (8)
Collaton St Mary CE (VA) Primary School, Paignton

Autumn - Cinquain

Autumn
Crushed leaves decay
Squirrels scaling high trees
Listen . . . the bird flapping his wings
Autumn.

Jessie Holmes-Brown (8)
Collaton St Mary CE (VA) Primary School, Paignton

Autumn - Cinquain

Autumn
Look, autumn's here
Birds whistling in the wind
The leaves crunching under your feet
It's gone . . .

Gabriella Morfey (8)
Collaton St Mary CE (VA) Primary School, Paignton

Autumn - Cinquain

Autumn,
Cherry-red leaves
Drifted down from the trees
Snapped, violently beneath your feet
Crunch, crunch.

Rebecca Jones (8)
Collaton St Mary CE (VA) Primary School, Paignton

Autumn - Cinquain

Autumn
Green leaves turn gold
On a moss-covered branch
The end of life is very near
Dying . . .

Rhiannon Jobes (8)
Collaton St Mary CE (VA) Primary School, Paignton

Autumn - Cinquain

Autumn
Killing summer
Then goes to wintertime
When little limpets of the spring
Begin.

Beau Jennians (8)
Collaton St Mary CE (VA) Primary School, Paignton

Autumn - Cinquain

Autumn
There and then gone
Rustling leaves in the cold
Summer has past, winter is near
Run fast.

Joe Killoran (8)
Collaton St Mary CE (VA) Primary School, Paignton

My Journey

It was so noisy that I heard
The roaring traffic rumble across my toes.

It was so calm that I saw
A slippery green frog jump across my feet
And leap onto a stone quickly.

It was so peaceful that I heard
The chime of the church bells.

It was so quiet that I saw
A gorgeous butterfly fly to gather pollen
From flower to flower.

Emily Hutchings (7)
Collaton St Mary CE (VA) Primary School, Paignton

My Sense Poem

It was so silent that I heard
Church bells chiming peacefully
It was so calm that I saw
A spider spinning a wonderful web
It was so quiet that I saw
A frog leaping along the riverbank
It was so peaceful that I heard
The wind blowing in the air
It was so peaceful that I could hear
The birds twittering in the pale blue sky.

Brendan Stacey (7)
Collaton St Mary CE (VA) Primary School, Paignton

My Journey

It was so quiet that I heard
The church bells ring.
It was so calm that I heard
The rushing frog leaping on the river bed.
It was so still that I saw
A spider spin its silky web.
It was so tranquil that I heard
A bird sing a beautiful song.
It was so noisy that all I heard
Was the thunder of the cars rushing down the road.

James Thom (8)
Collaton St Mary CE (VA) Primary School, Paignton

The Skyscraper

The towering skyscraper
In the middle of busy New York
Looking down like a huge giant
With thousands of glass eyes.

Hundreds of people rushing in and out
Like bees collecting honey
With eyes looking out with despair
Wishing they could break free.

Huge double doors
Letting people in and out
Like gateways to another realm
Between Heaven and Hell.

People running around like frenzied ants
Scavenging for money
But where is happiness
When peace and calm are out of sight?

Connor Smith (10)
Cubert School, Newquay

Summer

Summertime is here,
Diving off the pier,
Mummy eating sandwiches,
And Daddy drinking beer.

Waves growing higher,
Like a rising fire,
Dolphins swimming in and out,
Squirming like a massive trout.

Grampa reading a newspaper,
Granny falling asleep,
All the little grandchildren playing by their feet.

Zoë Pascoe (11)
Cubert School, Newquay

The Jungle

Tweeting, chirping, oohing, ahhing,
Birds and monkeys everywhere,
Ribbiting, rabbiting, leaping, lurching,
Frogs are green and bare.

Twitting, twooing, fluttering, flying,
Owls are hooting at night,
Shouting, shivering, calling, bawling,
The gorilla always in sight.

The noise of the jungle,
Is truly amazing,
The sights are just as good,
So if you ever go there,
Just make sure you look.

Michael White (11)
Cubert School, Newquay

The Great Rotweiller

A good pet
Tall, slim, strong
Like a warrior defending his master.
Fast as a cheetah
Running on and on.
Playful and cute.
The great dog is
A strong soldier.

Kyle Maywood (9)
Cubert School, Newquay

The Brilliant Eagle

The brilliant eagle,
Stalking as we speak,
Silent, vicious and eager,
Quiet as the blue sky.
Like the king of the air
It makes me feel worthless,
Like the boring sea
The brilliant eagle.

Steven Revell (11)
Cubert School, Newquay

The Mighty Lion

The mighty lion
Waving his golden mane.
Ravenous, strong, and ferocious
Like the king of the beasts.
As dangerous as death.
He makes me feel scared.
Like a tiny ant.
The mighty lion,
Predator of the world.

Patrick Davies (9)
Cubert School, Newquay

Autumn Leaves

Leaves falling to the ground
Rustling, what a peaceful sound
Leaves, golden, yellow and brown
Wrinkled, ridged and round.

Leaves falling, any place, anywhere
Changing from the colour green
Leaves falling off the trees
Anywhere, any place.

Lauren Coles (9)
Cubert School, Newquay

I Love Penguins

A lovely penguin
That dives into the dark blue sea.
Adorable, swirling penguins sliding along
Like so many fish in the sea.
I feel cold when I think about it.
I feel surprising inside.
A lovely penguin.
Everybody loves them.

Mollie O'Connor (10)
Cubert School, Newquay

Hallowe'en

The big pumpkin
Scary, fiery eyes
Glowing, expanding, bright
Like an expanding star
People knocking on your door
Excited over all the ghostly and witchy things
The big pumpkin
It goes on year after year.

Bethany Morey (10)
Cubert School, Newquay

Father Christmas

Father Christmas
Comes at night
Boys and girls
Cuddled tight.

Hooray, he's
At our house
We sleep so soundly
As a mouse.

Bells are ringing
Choirs are singing
Presents for girls and boys
Playing with new toys.

Miranda Robinson (10)
Cubert School, Newquay

The Streamlined Cheetah

The streamlined cheetah
Goes super fast
Speedy, quick, strong
Is like a scarlet Ferrari
As fast as lightning
It makes me feel envious of its speed
I feel as slow as a snail
The streamlined cheetah
Killer on the prowl.

Colbey Brook (10) & Robert Baxter (9)
Cubert School, Newquay

The Grazing Sheep

The grazing sheep
Constantly nibbling
Curly, fuzzy, matted
Like a summer's cloud
Like freshly cooked popcorn
Reminds me of summer
As warm as toast
The grazing sheep
Reminds me of warm, woolly jumpers.

Alex Burke (11)
Cubert School, Newquay

A Podgy Cat

A podgy cat
Always lying by the fire
Warm, thick and fluffy
As black as midnight
Shining like stars
I feel warm and sleepy
As small as an ant
A podgy cat
Makes me think of night.

Carys Jordan (9)
Cubert School, Newquay

The Cute Puppy

The cute puppy,
A very good pet,
Nosy, fast, fun,
Like a cuddly teddy bear,
As small as a pencil case,
It makes me feel big,
Like a big house everyone can see,
The cute puppy,
How loving we can be.

Thomas Adam Easterbrook (9)
Cubert School, Newquay

Volcanoes

The deep hole
Dormant and snoring
Rocky, sharp, dangerous
Like a sleeping giant
Growling like an empty stomach
It makes me feel nervous
Like a timid mouse
The deep hole
Forever dangerous.

Lucy Barkle (10)
Cubert School, Newquay

Horses

A piebald stands short and bold
Only 13hh
Plump, brown and white
As plump as a cherry tomato
As brown as an oak tree
So different but distinctive
As different as black and white
A piebald stands short and bold
A life of hacks.

Katie Wall (10)
Cubert School, Newquay

The Giant Tree

The giant tree
Was twice the size of me
As the days turned colder
And the nights grew darker
Without a doubt the trees are shaking in the breeze
As we are tucked up in bed nice and warm
This is what they said . . .
'We would love it if we could sleep in a comfy bed
Snug and hugging our ted.'

Jasmine Michell (10)
Cubert School, Newquay

The Dizzy Puppy

The dizzy puppy
Having a drink every second
Calm, cute, beautiful
Like a baby monkey crawling
As small as a one-month-old baby
She makes me feel tall
I feel as sweet as chocolate
The dizzy puppy
She makes me think of happy people.

Joanna Revell (9)
Cubert School, Newquay

The Giant Polar Bear

The giant polar bear
Colossal with a massive fluffy coat
Ravenous, brave and bold
Like an enormous white pompom
As vicious as a lion
It makes me feel like I've been skinned and I don't have any hair
Like a winter tree with no leaves on it
The giant polar bear
Starving throughout the years.

Hannah Jones (9)
Cubert School, Newquay

The Cute Puppy

The cute puppy
Love him, his hair is soft
Cute, cuddly and pretty
Like a big, bushy cloud
As white as a big, fluffy pillow
I feel happy he's alive
As happy as a hyena
The cute puppy
He makes me feel really calm.

Melissa Clemson (9)
Cubert School, Newquay

Hallowe'en

Hallowe'en,
Children trick or treating,
Adults not that keen,
People covered in sheeting.

Ghosts at their haunting,
They are sending a spooky howl,
Skeletons' insides flaunting,
A scary Simon Cowell.

Ella Ludlam (10)
Cubert School, Newquay

School

Monday
Get up and ready for school, *eugh!*
Remember, teachers, it's kids that rule.
Maths and English and history's cruel.
Eugh!

Tuesday
Get up and ready for school, *eugh!*
You're late and it's not your friends you've met.
Detention is exactly what you get.
Eugh!

Wednesday
Get up and have breakfast first, *eugh!*
Drink some juice to quench your thirst.
Dancing class, dances that we've rehearsed.
Eugh!

Thursday
Waking up early on a morning, *eugh!*
Art and science, really boring.
The rain outside is completely pouring.
Eugh!

Friday
Wake up very happy today, *yey!*
Skip to school and start to play.
Weekend tomorrow so a happy day.
Yey!

Joanne Hudspeth (10)
Cubert School, Newquay

The Dog And The Hedgehog

The dog and the hedgehog went on a cruise
On Titanic number three
They took a balloon to play with at noon
And hoped they'd arrive with glee.

Rebecca Billett (10)
Ellacombe Primary School, Torquay

Cinquain

Connor
Go get some milk
We have run out, OK?
But run or no breakfast for you
Bye-bye.

Maisy Wigington (10)
Ellacombe Primary School, Torquay

The Bird And The Warthog

The bird and the warthog went to New York
In a paper boat
They took a fork and their pet hawk
And hoped they would stay afloat.

Heather McIlveen (10)
Ellacombe Primary School, Torquay

The Monkey And The Donkey

The monkey and the donkey went to Mars
On a clapped-out bike made from brass
They took a flag
And a pink bag
That they took from the class.

Angellica Colman (10)
Ellacombe Primary School, Torquay

The Fish And The Rabbit

The fish and the rabbit went to Torquay
On a massive, jumping flea
They took a spade and a cake they made
So they could eat it with glee.

Kelsey Burns (10)
Ellacombe Primary School, Torquay

Tott'nham - Cinquain

Tott'nham
Oh great Tott'nham
You light up the football
You have great young passing players
Oh Spurs!

Connor Conneely (11)
Ellacombe Primary School, Torquay

Jack The Carthorse

Hoof-tapper
Tail-swisher
Carriage-puller
Leg-mover
Hay-eater
Day-worker
Night-sleeper
Friend-maker
Rain-sufferer
Neck-bender
Sharp-looker
Field-lover
Playful-player
Good-worker
Carrot-eater
Fast-runner
Stable-hater
Owner-lover.

Nicole Bloomfield (10)
Fremington Community Primary & Nursery School, Barnstaple

Morwellham Quay

We went to Morwellham Quay
It's about Victorian times you see
We had fun going down a mine
Then we went to make rope
Will I turn the handle? I hope
Then we went to a schoolhouse
I found a baby woodlouse
Inside it was very dark
We had lunch in a park
We didn't go on the ship
When we were down the mine I bashed my hip
The coach ride was very long
The coach went round the bend
But it was all worth it in the end
We didn't go to Life At Sea
I had a great time at Morwellham Quay.

Molly How (9)
Fremington Community Primary & Nursery School, Barnstaple

Morwellham Quay Copper Mine

On Thursday we went in a mine,
I thought it was fun and it was fine.
It wasn't scary although it was gloomy,
I didn't think it was very roomy.
In the mine it was quite damp,
Then Steve turned on all the lamps.
In the mine it was really narrow,
Then I thought I saw a sparrow.
All too soon it was time to go,
I remember well and enjoyed the show.

Cassie Dobert (9)
Fremington Community Primary & Nursery School, Barnstaple

Rope Making

String wind around, around, around,
Coil with each other, each other.
Twist to make a rope, make a rope,
Curl to make it thick, firm and strong.
Twine the golden material,
Pull it, make it twirl, make it twirl.
Tie a knot so it doesn't unravel,
Plait all strings together, together.
Handle turning cogs around,
Curling rope round, round, round.
Stretch, pull, tug and turn, tug and turn.
Stretch, stretch, pull, pull, tug, tug, turn, turn.
Complete and finished, now we have a
Golden, prickly and woody-smelling rope.

Katie Over (9)
Fremington Community Primary & Nursery School, Barnstaple

The Copper Mine

C opper mines are dark and scary,
O ur tour man was tall and hairy.
P oor people would be in the mine,
P oorer people wouldn't be fine.
E arly ages were not cool,
R ich children went to school.

M y visit
I n the mine was
N ot boring,
E verything was fine.

George Hopper (9)
Fremington Community Primary & Nursery School, Barnstaple

The Mine At Morwellham Quay

Under the ground at Morwellham Quay,
The setting is cold;
It's damp and musty.
We went in the mine,
Along the train line,
In the dark,
With a guide
And some dummies.

Esther Seaford (10)
Fremington Community Primary & Nursery School, Barnstaple

The Mine

Colder damper,
Water dripper,
Miner worker,
Tracker shaker,
Rocker breaker,
Copper finder.

Brianna Marshall (11)
Fremington Community Primary & Nursery School, Barnstaple

The Mine

Copper finder
Water dripper
Dummy creeper
Rock scraper
Cold shiverer.

Jack Hazell (11)
Fremington Community Primary & Nursery School, Barnstaple

The Ship

Boat starter
Ship darter
Sail steerer
Mist clearer
Deck cleaner
Smoke steamer
Loud speaker
Cannon seeker
Enemy shooter.

Alice Robotham (11)
Fremington Community Primary & Nursery School, Barnstaple

The Copper Miner

Rock knocker
Stone chipper
Copper nicker
Digger deeper
Tunnel blaster
Ore taker.

Luke Cornish (10)
Fremington Community Primary & Nursery School, Barnstaple

The Copper Mine Rhyme

In the mine at Morwellham Quay,
It was funny, dark and lots to see.
Like dummies, rocks, diggers that pound.
The ride was bumpy, deep underground!
Then . . .
Out of the mine weather: moderate and fine.

Nicole Lathwell (10)
Fremington Community Primary & Nursery School, Barnstaple

The Mine

The train ride was wet,
I started to fret,
Chugga-clank, chugga-clank
It was dark
When we parked
Chugga-clank, chugga-clank
But by the end
It was fun!
People scared?
There were none!
Chugga-clank, chugga-clank
Chugga-clank, chugga-clank.

Zac Everest (10)
Fremington Community Primary & Nursery School, Barnstaple

Victorian School

Victorian schools, trust me
You wouldn't want to go!
Clean hands, clean fingernails as well.
Girls got whipped on their palms,
Boys on the backs of their hands.
'Don't slouch, little miss!'
Writing done on slates, slate pencils too.
On their knees they had to write.
Six hours a day, no fun at all,
From the age of three,
'Til the age of eight.

Courtney Jewell (9)
Fremington Community Primary & Nursery School, Barnstaple

Miners

Good-worker
Job-hater
Money-earner
Excellent-pusher
Copper-finder
Tin-finder
Good-digger
Dynamite-user
Dark-lover
Pasty-eater.

Ross Bayliss (10)
Fremington Community Primary & Nursery School, Barnstaple

Jack The Carthorse At Morwellham Quay

People-amuser
Steady-walker
Victorian-traveller
Pat-wanter
Hoof-rester
Rein-jolter
Head-tosser
Carriage-puller
Tail-swisher.

Rachael Gatehouse (9)
Fremington Community Primary & Nursery School, Barnstaple

Miners

Back-breaker
Harsh-cougher
Rock-obliterator
Copper-uncoverer
Sweat-producer
Money-earner
Water-devourer
Pasty-swallower
Dynamite-applier.

Oliver Sharp (10)
Fremington Community Primary & Nursery School, Barnstaple

Victorian School

Fingernail-inspector
Candle-lighter
Good-handwriter
Cane-user
Silent-worker
Lesson-learner
Chalk-scraper.

Molly Hayden (9)
Fremington Community Primary & Nursery School, Barnstaple

George And Charlotte - Copper Mine

Dark-placer
Young-worker
Thin passageway-mover
Wheelbarrow-pusher
Daylight-seeker
Eight-hourer
Poison-user
Pasty-eater
Copper-getter.

Kimberley Morgan (10)
Fremington Community Primary & Nursery School, Barnstaple

The Mine At Morwellham

T ime has come to go into the mine,
H eat of earth vanished but not underground,
E vil dummies stare

M ighty rocks pressing down from above,
 I n the mine the water drips,
N asty, slimy fear that grips,
E qually as cold as snow.

Callum Parsley (10)
Fremington Community Primary & Nursery School, Barnstaple

L O Alliteration In Poetry

One wicked witch.
Two terrible twins.
Three thin fish.
Four fiery, flickering flames.
Five funny, flirting clowns.
Six smarting stones.
Seven shiny shells.
Eight funny fish.
Nine nosy neighbours.
Ten terrible teachers.

Kalli Hewings-Pollard (7)
Gerrans School, Truro

Love

Love is like a heart in the sunset
It tastes like strawberry-pink ice cream
Love feels like cuddly, soft clouds
It smells like a red rose
It looks like juicy, red lips
It sounds like a loud, crackling firework
It feels warm and cosy like cotton wool.

Alice Hooper (7)
Gerrans School, Truro

The Environmentalist's Poem

The wetness of water
Is the sogginess of the sea,
Rough or smooth
No end there be.
Eternal blueness
And grey and green,
And with all our pollution
It's so unclean.

Oh uncontrollable life-giver
Oh sea! Oh sea!
Oh silvery big slither
Oh sea! Oh sea!

Though we try to protect you
Destroying you we are,
And with all your life
That will be terrible by far.
You give us food
And life and fame,
And we try to protect you
As it's not a game.

Oh uncontrollable life-giver
Oh sea! Oh sea!
Oh silvery big slither
Oh sea! Oh sea!

Nathaniel Keymer (10)
Gerrans School, Truro

The Sea

The sea is as blue as a bluebell,
The sea is as rough as the jagged cliffs,
The sea is as smooth as silk,
The sea is as uncontrollable as life,
The sea can be as horrible as a demon.

Isaac Bryan (9)
Gerrans School, Truro

The Sea

The sea is as smooth as silk
The sea is as shiny as glistening silver
Yawning deep is the sea
Boats fill the harbour
Like fruit in a bowl
The sea is as rough as a storm.

Jack Clifford Wing (9)
Gerrans School, Truro

My World

One wet, windy winter
Two terrible tigers
Three lovely, lickable lollies
Four dancing, prancing dolphins
Five flipping, flying falcons
Six running, rasping runners
Seven big bananas
Eight crunching, killing cobras
Nine great gorillas
Ten tall teachers.

Joel Keymer (8)
Gerrans School, Truro

Hate

Hate is red like bright, flowing blood,
It tastes like hot, spicy curry,
Hate smells like burning matches,
Hate looks like flaming fire in the distance,
It sounds like angry, noisy shouting,
It feels like a rough, ridged stone.

Abigail Little (8)
Gerrans School, Truro

Colours

Yellow is bright sunshine
Yellow is hot, burning light
Yellow is a golden watch
Yellow is soft, gleaming sand

Red is a sparkling jewel
Red is school book bags
Red is gleaming jewels in the sand
Red is Liverpool's wonderful shirt

Green is short, flowing grass in summer
Green is thin, spiky leaves on a palm tree
Green is bright lily pads on a pond
Green is frogs leaping out of water.

Callum Grahamslaw (7)
Gerrans School, Truro

Colours

Yellow is a tasty, soft banana
Yellow is a shooting, streaking meteorite
Yellow is a bronze statue from the past
Yellow is a tennis ball striking through the wind

Red is a dragon breathing red-hot fire
Red is a studded football boot
Red is the top colour of the rainbow
Red is falling leaves in autumn

Green is fields in the distance
Green is yachts going through the mist
Green is army clothes
Green is the cool, rough grass.

Thomas Chater & Callum (7)
Gerrans School, Truro

Alliteration In My Number Poem

One flying, fit fish.
Two tall, towering trees.
Three silly, soft sausages.
Four fat, funny fish.
Five pink, snorting piggies.
Six dancing, darting ducks.
Seven jumping, jiving Jacks.
Eight happy, hopping hamsters.
Nine naughty, nutty newts.
Ten singing, twinkling salmon.

Richard Chaffin (8)
Gerrans School, Truro

The Sea And My Senses

It looks like a rough, rapid herd of elephants charging towards me.
It sounds like a big drum crashing against the jagged rocks.
It tastes like sea salts.
It smells like sea salts.
It is as curly and wavy as your hair.
The colour is like an inky-blue, purple as a plum, green as moss.
The sea is my nutshell.

Jade Kneebone (11)
Gerrans School, Truro

Fear

Fear is like a big furry monster
It tastes like disgusting meat bones
It smells rotten and bitter
It looks like blue, flashing, bright lights
It sounds like booming thunder
It feels rough like the edge of paper.

Francesca Williams (7)
Gerrans School, Truro

The Ocean

On a rough day the waves
Are like curling grass

The sea is as blue as the ink
Flushing out your pen

The sea can be as uncontrollable
As a herd of bulls

The sea is as loud as
Trolls quarrelling

The sea is as fast
As racing horses

The sea feels like
A silk dress

The sea is as shiny
As diamond rings

The rocks are like swords
Striking out of the floor

But on a flat day
The sea is like a freshly made bed

Just a few little ripples

It can be flat one minute and wavy the next
But it is still fun to swim in.

Elliott Little (10)
Gerrans School, Truro

The Sea

As smooth as glass
As shiny as a silver fish
The bass are glistening in the sunlight
The sea is calm and warm
It smashes against the harbour wall like cymbals.

Kyran Hooper (9)
Gerrans School, Truro

The Sea

There's a little sailing boat out on the sea
The broken, the boisterous,
The bumpy sea.

There's a little sailing boat out on the sea
The ferocious, the fierce,
The free sea.

There's a little sailing boat out on the sea
The disordered, the demented,
The disastrous sea.

There's a little sailing boat out on the sea
The crafted, the carved,
The scoped sea.

There's a little sailing boat out on the sea
The lawless, the larking,
The longing sea.

Christopher Thomas (11)
Gerrans School, Truro

The Sea

It looks like the swells are
Hills of shiny glitter
Moving along the water

But suddenly the hills
Turn into mounts
Roaring and crashing
Down onto the beach
As uncontrollable
As a hurricane
Spinning out of
Control and hungry
For destruction.

Izaak Jones (10)
Gerrans School, Truro

The Sea

The drops are like rain
As cold as ice
Like a bumpy road
The soft sea tickles my toes
Stamping in the water
Wind comes, boats turn
And when I touch the water with my hand
It feels like a storm coming.

David Kneebone (9)
Gerrans School, Truro

The Sea

As shiny as golden bars
As smooth as glass
As rough as jagged rocks
As fast as a speeding bullet
Drips running off the water skis
Leaving a vapour trail of bubbles behind
Flying over the splashing, crashing waves.

James Chater (9)
Gerrans School, Truro

The Sea

The sea tastes like salt which I taste even when I'm on a boat.
The sea sounds like little bits of glass
Smashing on the floor with a loud crash.
The sea feels like gushes of wind.
The sea smells like seaweed.
The sea looks like a blue, moving, stained glass window.

Daniel Vanson (9)
Gerrans School, Truro

The Sea

As shiny as silver,
As rough as a storm,
As blue as a bluebird,
As calm as a puddle on the road,
As green as a green forest,
As curly as curly hair,
As clean as blowing wind,
As uncontrollable as a fast car,
As full of food as a larder.
It makes me as happy as a baby with a lollipop.
It's as ripply as a raisin,
As furious as a lion,
As smooth as pebbles,
As never-ending as life.
The sea is a great thing in the world.

Nicholas Smith (9)
Gerrans School, Truro

The Sea And Me

My mum and me love the sea like a hedgehog with its spikes.
We can't be pulled away from it but it feels as cold as ice.
The sea is as soft as a kitten.
The sea is as smooth as pebbles.
If me and my mum were pulled away from the sea
It would make me and my mum very unhappy.
The sea is as wet and soggy as a newborn puddle.
Creatures live in it and so do rocks.
Crashing against the crippled rocks it makes the sand's family.
The sea feeds us and is very blue.
It is clear on a good day.
It is churned up like milk being made into cheese.
All my family loves the sea.

Abigail Langridge (10)
Gerrans School, Truro

The Sea

I look out to sea and find
Wonderful colours, blue, green,
And in a sunset, red, orange and yellow.

Calm, smooth like an egg,
Then craggy as a bush.
Blue as a bluebell, yet in a sunset,
Red as blood.

It was smooth as silk,
Then rough as a zip undone.
It's as cold as ice,
Even when outside it's as hot as fire.

The sea smells like seaweed and dead fish,
It sounds like china being dropped on the floor,
Or books being smacked on a wall,
The sea tastes like sour oranges.
Sometimes it smells like rotten fruit.

I love the sea.

Charlotte Breckin (9)
Gerrans School, Truro

Sea

It is as wavy as your hair
It is as silvery as tinfoil
It is as silent as a mouse
It is as blue as bluebells.

You hear the seagulls calling
Over the glistening sea
You can hear children playing
In the surging sea.

It smells like dried seaweed
It smells like clean washing
You can smell the salt moving in the sea.

Rachel Thomas (9)
Gerrans School, Truro

Loneliness

Loneliness is a tiny fish in a huge sea.
It tastes like burnt toast
And smells of bubbles.
The sound of ears popping.
It feels like being in a big bubble!

Katie Hill (10)
Grenville College Junior School, Bideford

Happiness

Happiness is light pink
It tastes like ripe strawberries
And smells like perfume
Happiness is caramel chocolate melting
The sound of birds tweeting
It feels fresh!

Abbie Loka (9)
Grenville College Junior School, Bideford

Happiness

Happiness is pink
It tastes like cake
And smells like lemons
Happiness is beautiful
The sound of a lullaby
Happiness is special.

Lucy Palmer (10)
Grenville College Junior School, Bideford

Happiness

Happiness is all bright colours
It tastes like caramel dipped in marshmallow
And smells like fresh air
Happiness is playing
The sound of bouncing on a trampoline
It feels like the best football in the world.

Nevin Cox (9)
Grenville College Junior School, Bideford

Happiness

Happiness is yellow
It tastes like chocolate
And smells like sugar
Happiness is a baby kitten
The sound of birds tweeting
Happiness is a child in the park.

Oliver Bailey Coombs (9)
Grenville College Junior School, Bideford

Anger

Anger is a scorching flame destroying everything in its path.
It tastes like gravel grazing the back of your throat.
It smells like burning lilies.
Anger is a treacherous fiend.
The sound of a million atomic bombs going off inside your head.
It feels like a terrible whirlwind inside your heart.
Anger.

Noah Bodinetz (10)
Grenville College Junior School, Bideford

Confusion

Confusion is a hurricane
It tastes like nothingness
And smells like cider fresh from the orchard
Confusion is a whirlpool of thoughts
The sound of lots of shouting out at once
It feels like ice going down your back.

Michael Taylor (9)
Grenville College Junior School, Bideford

Anger

Anger is death
It tastes like red wine
And smells like dead roses
Anger is red blood
The sound of someone dying
It feels like shivers down my spine.

Adam Hughes (9)
Grenville College Junior School, Bideford

Anger

Anger is a reckless hurricane
Anger tastes like gunpowder
Anger smells like a fired bullet
Anger is war
Anger sounds like a battle behind you
Anger feels like a dagger scraped down your back.

Charlie Woolcott (9)
Grenville College Junior School, Bideford

Anger

Anger is a monstrous demon
It tastes like cold blood
And smells like a rotting corpse
Anger is a fiery hell of infernos
Anger is the sound of a woman screaming
Anger feels like rough, unbreakable scales.

Xavier Veillet (9)
Grenville College Junior School, Bideford

Emotion Poem

Happiness is a jelly bean
It tastes like chocolate
And smells like pink roses
Happiness is to smile
The sound of a pink fire
Happiness feels like snow.

Emma Richards (10)
Grenville College Junior School, Bideford

Sleepiness

Sleepiness is sky-blue
It tastes like puffing bubbles
And smells like a drip of water.
Sleepiness is a dream
The sound of a clear river flowing.
Sleepiness, it feels like sunbathing on a hot day.

Sam Tithecott (9)
Grenville College Junior School, Bideford

Anger

Anger is a steaming volcano
It tastes like raw chicken
It smells like human guts
Anger is your brain bursting
The sound of a reckless devil
It feels like aliens pulling out your eyeballs.

Thomas Hyam (9)
Grenville College Junior School, Bideford

Pick 'N' Mix

Zebra, panda, chimpanzee
What can you make out of all three?
Zebda, panra, zepanzee
This is what you get out of all three!

Ladybug, owl, cat, beehive
What do you get if you cross all five?
Ladat, beowl, cal, bughive
This is what you get if you cross all five!

Seagull, falcon, eagle, condor
What do you get if you mix all four?
Eacon, seagor, falgull, eagor
This is what you get if you mix all four!

Bee, cow, dog, ant, spider, ticks
What do you get if you twist all six?
Bew, dant, spee, anticks
This is what you get if you twist all six!

Pig or goat, the rest is up to you
If anyone deserves to do this, you do
Come on and join in, you
Do it now, do it now, now do!

Matthew Bone (10)
Heamoor CP School, Penzance

Tiger

Tiger, I saw you sprinting,
Sprinting for your prey.

Eyes looking, looking like a
Volcanic flame.

Tiger, I saw you sprinting,
Sprinting for your prey.

Teeth as sharp as a
Spanish sword.

Tiger, I saw you sprinting,
Sprinting for your prey.

Body striped like an orange
And black flag.

Tiger, I saw you sprinting,
Sprinting for your prey.

Luke Jenkin (10)
Heamoor CP School, Penzance

A Teacher

The teacher is the weirdest creature of all,
Sometimes it likes to make absurd speeches in the hall.
Its habitat is on the moon,
With its mighty, trusted spoon.
The sound it makes is very strange,
It's a squeaky voice that comes in every different range.
It looks exactly like a human man,
But look closely, it has a very odd green tan.
Its appetite is very fishy,
As its diet is cheese and onion crisps
With children that are squishy.
Now you have heard all about the teacher,
I'm sure you'll find it a very weird creature.
So now promise me
To keep away from this absurd he or she!

Scarlett Cohen (9)
Heamoor CP School, Penzance

Sports Car Began

Sports car began
She got her roar from the thunder
She got her rumble from the volcano
And she made her sound

At breakfast
She got her fastness from a cheetah
She got her swiftness from a jaguar
And she had her speed

At lunch
She took her tint from a chameleon
That camouflaged itself in different places
Then she had her colour

At dinner
She got her muscle power from a lion
Running free
And she had her strength

And sports car was made.

Ben Hardy (9)
Heamoor CP School, Penzance

Owl Began

Light bulbs switch on and off for his eyes.
Ears hidden beneath his feathers.
Turning his head like a marble ball rolling across the floor.
Feet clap together catching his prey.
Hoot-hoot.
Mist of the night, crystal spiderwebs hang in the oak tree.

Louisa Bonner (10)
Heamoor CP School, Penzance

Crazy Creatures

A pack of wolves chasing a penguin
What a one-sided race.
The editor's chasing the reporter
Swinging a huge mace.

A monkey chasing a lion
What is this all about?
The editor is chasing the reporter
And slapping him with a trout.

A fish attacking a whale
This is very strange!
The reporter escaped the editor
What a very nice change.

The editor thinks the reporter
Is a nincompoop!
But now the reporter is ready
Because he's friends with army troop.

Robert Dunn (11)
Heamoor CP School, Penzance

What Am I?

Claws - bent as moons.
Teeth - sharp as the tops of cocoons.
Legs - stiff as bamboos.
Eyes - beady, black as night.
Face - round as the Earth.
Ears - pointed, they're alert -
Do you know what I am?

Shannen Louise Stringer (10)
Heamoor CP School, Penzance

Tortoise Began

Tortoise began
He took the apple tree log
He took the mud from the ground
And made his colour.

He took the tennis ball in the air
He took the polystyrene cup
To make his legs.

He took the green grass
He took the moss from the tree
And made his tail.

He took the frog from the pond
He took the book from the floor
And made his size.

He took the tiles from the ground
He took the spikes from the nail
Which made his shell.

He took the person's elbow
He took the shop's watch
To make his arms.

Oliver Jack Marston (9)
Heamoor CP School, Penzance

Fox Awakes

Blazing fire like a red-hot oven,
A coat like a devil's fork.

Eyes like never-ending sky,
They sparkle like a twinkling star.

A tail like a coconut sea,
And a soft tail like grass.

Go on run, fox, catch your prey,
Run like the wind!

Grace Carter (10)
Heamoor CP School, Penzance

Platypus Began

He snatched the richness of the soil
As soft as sparkly diamond silk.
He seized the shine of the waterproof river coat.
    That's how he got his fur.

For his tail he grasped the dead of autumn leaves,
The scratches of a sharp carving knife
And the glistening sparkle of the moonlight.
    That's how he got his tail.

At dawn he clutched the blackness of night
And he stole the silk web from a black widow.
He caught the tumbling waves in the sea.
    That's how he got his feet.

At midnight he grabbed the dark winter's day.
He stole the crusher of ice, it opened like the sunrise.
    That's how he got his beak.

Duck-billed platypus was created.

Adam Prowse & George Jackson (10)
Heamoor CP School, Penzance

Polar Bear Began

For his fur he stole the softest cloud you can imagine.
His ears are as pointy as sticks.
He lives on the cold ice of Antarctica
And eats like a hungry shark.

His wet nose is as soft as snow.
His eyes light up bright as a car.
His claws look like tigers' teeth.
Polar bear began.

Jasmine Rayner (10) & Jamie-Leigh Lobb
Heamoor CP School, Penzance

The Giant Squid

They swiped the shape of a spear point.
They chose the colour of the peach.
They uncovered two pitch-black ovals
And so the head was formed.

They grasped ten thousand toilet plungers
The size of an eye
The hue of flesh.
The suckers created.

They found strings of long spaghetti
Squashed at the ends.
The tentacles made.

By now you may have guessed
Or maybe you haven't.
The animal is the giant squid
And that is that
So there.

Drew Maguire (10)
Heamoor CP School, Penzance

Parrot Began

The hook of a scimitar
The colours of a rainbow
The sharpness of a knife
Formed his beak.

Feathers like a passion flower
The green of leaves
Blue from the sea.

He took his webbed feet
From the colour of his head.
He took the roughness of his foot
From the bark of the oak tree.

Chloe Carley & Kerryanne Taylor (10)
Heamoor CP School, Penzance

Fairy Begins

In spring fairy begins.
For her wings
She took the pink flowers
From the forest.
At night she took the stars
From the moonlit sky.

In summer for her hair
She took the gold from the sun.
She took the softness of
The cotton wool.

In autumn for her clothes
She took the leaves from the
Acorn tree.
She took the leaves from the
Fern.

In winter for her personality
She took the passion from the
Passion flower.
She took the thunder from the
Dark sky.

Beth Marshall (9)
Heamoor CP School, Penzance

Untitled

It scratched the desert-coloured sand for its fur.
Its eyes from the sight of the light of the sun.
It got its pads by making the colour of the night sky
And spreading the dirt.

It captured its bounce by coiling the spring from a bouncy castle.
That's how a kangaroo began.

Jordan Johnstone (9)
Heamoor CP School, Penzance

The Start Of The Peacock

At dawn it captured the sun's gaze,
Its tail opened out like a Chinese fan,
It seized the concentration of many eyes
For its tail.

It stole the shininess of marbles,
The black of midnight
And the beads of a necklace
For its mysterious eyes.

It grabbed the duck's webbed feet,
The silver of moonlight
And the blaze of the shiny sun
For its feet

And that's how the peacock was formed.

Rhys Brownfield (11) & Oliver Angove (10)
Heamoor CP School, Penzance

Red Squirrel Began

Red squirrel began
He took the deepest sunset
The softness of the sand
And the finest grass
For his fur.

For his tail
He stole the lion's mane
And the movement of a spider monkey.

In winter he snatched
The whiteness of the snow
And the sparkle from the stars
For his teeth

And so red squirrel began.

Marcel Torode (10)
Heamoor CP School, Penzance

Swan Emerges

She stole the midnight sky,
The ocean sway
And the darkness of the blackest cave for her eye.

She took the colour of the sunset
And the shape of a pyramid
To create her beak.

She snatched the grace of the wind that blows
And the push of a swing
To satisfy her movement.

At dawn she captured the smoothness of a polar bear,
The flexibility of a piece of elastic
For her neck.

And so, after a long day
Swan emerged.

Daisy Jenkins (10)
Heamoor CP School, Penzance

Owl Began!

For his eyes he stole the brightness of the traffic light
He snatched the glitter of the moonlight
And the roundness of marbles
And owl made his eyes.

He borrowed the letter c
The sharpness of a point of a pencil
And he made his claws.

At dawn he stole the horn of a train
For his voice.

And owl was made!

Hannah Griffith (10)
Heamoor CP School, Penzance

Monkey Began

Monkey began
He took the brown from the muddy rivers
He took his yellow eyes from the moon
To make his face

For his tail
He took the long, curly branches off a tree
Which wave about in the wind
Like long, curling arms

For his breakfast
He took the golden colour of the sun
With its burning fire
To get his bananas

From the black bear he took his mouth
He took his smile from the grey mouse
For his voice he stole the letters from the alphabet.

That's how monkey was made.

Breon Day-Nicholls (9)
Heamoor CP School, Penzance

Cheetah's Wars

He stole the colour of sand
And the blackness of the depths
Of the ocean to make his fur.

He snatched the skill of many,
Many fighters for his deadly hunt.

He grabbed the zoom of a bullet,
The stealth of a secret agent.

He seized the blade of dead wars
For his mighty teeth.

Stefan Osborne & George Mitchell (10)
Heamoor CP School, Penzance

Dragonfly Began

In the summer
She took the dark blue from the sea.
She took the light blue from the sky
And made her colour.

At school
She took the child's pencil.
She took the teacher's finger
And made her shape.

In the wood
She took the horse's hair.
She took the twig from a tree
And she made her legs.

In the field
She took the buzzing bee.
She took the whisper from the blowing wind
And she made her sound.

In Neverland
She took the fluttering tooth fairy.
She took the soft leaves
And she made her wings.

Lauren Date (9)
Heamoor CP School, Penzance

Tiger Began

Tiger borrowed the orangeness of the sun
And the blackness of the night
And tiger made his fur

Tiger snatched the crescent of the moon
And the sharpness of thorns
And tiger made his claws

For tiger's eyes he stole the glitter of car lights

And tiger was created.

Lauren Ridge (10)
Heamoor CP School, Penzance

Elephant Began

He took his tusks from
The Devil's horns

He took his voice from
Thunder and lightning

He took his ears from
The bottom of the boat

He took his shape from
A humpback whale

He took his long legs from
A giraffe

He took his trunk from
A didgeridoo

And elephant was made.

Ryan Hosken (9)
Heamoor CP School, Penzance

Leopard Began!

On the hot, sunny plains of Africa
He stole the blackness of the night
And the waviness of the sea
And he made his spots.

He seized the shininess of the stars
And the roundness of the moon
And he made his eyes.

He snatched the whiteness of the snow,
The sharpness of knives
And he made his teeth.

And that was how leopard was made.

Izzy Williams (10)
Heamoor CP School, Penzance

Locust Began

Locust began
He took the spindliness of a book page
He took the bendiness of string
And made his legs

At breakfast time
He took the transparency of a window
He took the clearness of crystal
For his wings

At lunch
He took the length of a spider's leg
He took the fineness of human hair
To make his antennae

At dinner time
He took the shape of a mine shaft
He took the plumpness of a ripened fruit
And made his body

At supper
He took the death of the gun
He took the heat of the sun
For his plague

And locust was made.

Olaf Marshall Whitley (9)
Heamoor CP School, Penzance

Elephant Began

For its sharpness of its tusks it took a carving knife.
It stole a roll of an enormous rock for its movement.
At dawn it captured a horn for its trunk
Spraying water for thirst.

And elephant was created.

Rebecca Ingram (10)
Heamoor CP School, Penzance

Human Being Began

Human being began
She took the roundness of a circle
She took the bottom of a pine tree
To make her hands

She took the meat of pasties
She took the handle of the brush
To make her arms

She took the shape of a football
She took the shape of the oranges
To make her eyes

She took the sausage from the freezer
She took the trunk of a tree
To make her legs

She took the bottom of a drum
She took the measuring cup from the kitchen
To make her neck

She took the knight's sword
She took the horns of the Devil
To make her skeleton

Human being began.

Kerenza Mitchell (9)
Heamoor CP School, Penzance

Leopard Began

Leopard began
He rolled in the mud
He rolled in the yellow paint
For his coat

In Greece
He took the quickness of the car
He took the swiftness of the Olympic champion
To make his speed

In England
He took the form of the dog
He took the outline of the cat
For his shape

At the seaside
He took the rope of the sail
He took the tough string of the swing
To make his tail

In Africa
He took the legs of the jaguar
He took the branches of the tree
To make his legs

Leopard began.

Merrion Steer (9)
Heamoor CP School, Penzance

Black Widow Spider Began

Black widow spider began
She took the blackness of the night sky
She took the redness of blood
And made her colour

From the tailor
She took the stickiness of glue
She took the softness of silk
To make her web

From China
She took the sharpness of samurai swords
And took the curves of semi-circles
And made her fangs

From the beach
She took the roundness of a beach ball
And she took the fattiness of Fatty from the Beano
To make her abdomen.

From the maths lesson
She took the shortness of pencils
She took the six sides of a hexagon
And made her legs.

From the garden
She took three ants side by side
She took a snail
To make her size

In the darkness of night
She took the deadliness of the panther
She took the greenness of urine
To make her venom

And black widow spider was made.

Harry Eden Trezona (9)
Heamoor CP School, Penzance

Kitten Began

Kitten began
She took the long, thin felt-tip pen
She took rolled up paper
And made her legs.

At one o'clock
She took the tummy from Piglet
She took the shape of the sweet tube
And made her body.

At two o'clock
She took the puffiness from the cushion
She took the softness of hair
And made her fur.

At three o'clock
She took the darkness from the black crayon
She took the black paint
And made her colour.

At four o'clock
She took the twisted screw
She took the sharp pencil
And made her claws.

At five o'clock
She took the dog's lead
She took the ruler
And made her tail

At six o'clock
Kitten was made.

Shannon Moseley (9)
Heamoor CP School, Penzance

Goat Began

Goat began
For her horns
She stole from the Devil.
She took the sparkle from the unicorn.

She took the brown from the muddy river.
She took the grey from a stone
And made her colour.

For her tail
She took the root from the tree.
Took the twig off the wood's ground.

She took the trotters of a pig.
She took the hooves from Pan, king of the forest
To make her hooves.

To make her beard
She took the silk from a spider's web.
She took the seeds from a dandelion clock

And goat was made.

Jasmine Hannah Huckle (9)
Heamoor CP School, Penzance

Fast Man!

Wheels so slick and smooth
Don't blink or you'll miss it move!
The engine roaring like thunder
Rocketing under and under
The wing cutting through the air
Going so fast it'll give you a scare
The colours from the rainbow
This machine doesn't go slow
At the end of the bonnet
We can go supersonic
This car flies like a bird
With an engine that sure can be heard.

Steven Platts (9)
Heamoor CP School, Penzance

Koala Began

At breakfast time
He took the slowness of the sloth
He took the tiredness of the turtle
To make his movement

At lunchtime
He took the bracken from the trees
He took the softness of the sheepskin
To make his coat

At teatime
He took the head of a teddy bear
He took the strength of a walrus
To make his shape

At bedtime
He took the greyness of clay
He took the blackness of burnt branches
To make his colour

And koala was made.

Billy Read (9)
Heamoor CP School, Penzance

Battleaxe Began

Battleaxe began
He took the metal from the deepest, darkest mine.
He took the wood from the tree.
He took the strength of the ox.
He took the might of the elephant.
He took the shape from the signpost.
He took the accuracy of a bullet.
He took the precision of a sharpened flint.
He gripped it with a fistful of anger.
He held it ready for attack.

Jack James (9)
Heamoor CP School, Penzance

The Penguin's New Beginning

For the penguin's colour of darkness
It snatched the colour of midnight
At dawn it stole the whiteness of the moonlight,
For its golden chest it speared the glint of yellow
And snatched the sunlight.

At dawn it seized the orange
For its sharp, pointy beak.
For the point it took the cobra's
Sharp and narrow fang.
After stealing the cobra's fang
It stole the lion's crunch.

For the glistening and shiny eye
It clutched the sparkling star.
For its blue pupil
It stole the clear, blue sky.
At dawn it nipped
The big and bold hoop earrings
For the amazing shape.

For its movement it grabbed the toy car
And discovered the slide.
At dawn it snatched the waddle
From the little waddling duck.
The penguin managed to find out how
To swim from Ollie the Otter.

Matthew Quick & Jamie Dennis (10)
Heamoor CP School, Penzance

Creatures In The Ocean

In the deep blue sea live
Dolphins jumping up to the sky
Lots of sea horses bobbing by
Schools of fish shimmer along
Listening to the mermaid's song
Sharks hunting for their food
Jellyfish wobble, they're in a good mood
Penguins fly in the ocean so deep
Seals twist and turn and even leap
Oh I wish I lived in the deep blue sea.

Ella MacPhee (10)
Lady Seaward's School, Exeter

Chelsea Is My Team

Codie Wilson is my name
Football is my favourite game
Chelsea is my favourite team
This is my biggest dream
Look over your shoulder
Because when I am older
You could be watching me on TV
With my favourite team Chelsea.

Codie Wilson (9)
Lady Seaward's School, Exeter

Dragon's Flaming

Dragon's raging with fire,
Flying higher and higher.

What a furnace, will it burn us
With a rage of its flaming furnace?

Climbing faster, *flash!* It's back
Burning villages with its fiery furnace.

Shane Thomas Dougan (11)
Lady Seaward's School, Exeter

This Is Just To Say I Have Sold The House

This is just to say
I have sold
The house
That was in
The city

And which
You were probably
Saving
For shelter

Forgive me
They were rich
So nice
And so happy.

Oliver Cassidy-Butler (10)
Lady Seaward's School, Exeter

Animania

Monkey swinging from tree to tree,
Tiger cubs playing happily,
Snakes slithering on the ground,
Elephants plodding round and round,
Skunks smelling really bad,
Turtles looking very sad,
Giraffes eating all the leaves,
Lions doing as they please,
Kangaroos jumping really high,
Squirrels climbing towards the sky,
Bats sleeping all day long,
Birds singing a tuneful song.

Alice Elizabeth Johnson (10)
Lady Seaward's School, Exeter

The Wakening

The house for me, the house for you,
In the dusty attic, 'neath number two
The house for you was the house for me -
A treasure map that I want you to see

Start at Cut Purse Corner
Where two sovereigns greet the day
One shall line your pocket
The other point the way

Follow then her finger
Until the church you reach
Look inside the graveyard
For the angel who did teach

Examine with great caution
Examine with great stealth
For one wing leads to nothing
The other leads to wealth

Proceed in this direction
For ten score yards and three
Ignoring all obstruction
Until you reach the tree

Climb into its branches
Heaven awaits you there
A fork that never graced a table
Holds the costliest fare.

One is dead but not forgotten
A name lived on when the body was rotten
One is forgotten but not dead
Which Tom Tiddler is in your head?

Jamie May (11)
Lady Seaward's School, Exeter

The River

The water is still and calm.
You can see your reflection
Softly going by.
Pretty and calmly,
Flowing along,
Waiting until it gets pushed down the waterfall
With the other waves.

The water is crashing,
Swirling and whirling down the waterfall,
Cutting away at the rocks and pebbles,
As it falls down,
And crashes and smashes
At the bottom of the waterfall.

The river is rushing along.
You can see your reflection
Rushing past.
Going as fast as a jet.

Kirsty Sutton (8)
Manor Primary School, Ivybridge

The River

Rushing, frothing,
Smashing against the rocks.
Bubbling, oozing,
Plunging and brimming,
Crashing and running,
Eating and swirling,
Splashing,
Eroding,
Raging water.

Freddie Monk & Ellie Smith (7)
Manor Primary School, Ivybridge

My River

Flying river
Twisting and turning,
Eroding rocks.
Swaying river
Swirling and whirling,
Speeding river
Eating water.

Babbling rocks,
Rippling waterfall,
Rocks falling,
Foaming froth,
Wild river,
Flying rocks.
Cutting and eating,
Chewing and cutting,
My monster river.

George Turns (7)
Manor Primary School, Ivybridge

My River

Pushing and leaping,
Rushing and rippling,
My river.
See-through water,
Reflections in it.
Trees swaying,
Down the waterfall.
Splashing and bubbling,
Plunging, swirling and bumping
Goes my river.

Charlotte Stemp (8)
Manor Primary School, Ivybridge

The River

The water was falling,
Crashing, swirling, whirling,
Eating away at the stones.
The water was swaying,
Over the stones
And rocks.
The river was rushing,
Down the waterfall.
It would go flowing down to the sea,
Crashing all the way.
Going faster and faster,
All the way down.
In the sea
The water would sway,
Side to side,
All salty and horrible to drink,
You can almost see your reflection.

Jasmin Bird (8)
Manor Primary School, Ivybridge

The River

Falling and foaming,
Eating and eroding,
Rushing and gushing,
Crashing and cutting,
Falling and thundering,
Rippling and reflecting,
Water falling and crashing,
Flicking and flinging,
The water is so cold.

Kai Whelbourne (8)
Manor Primary School, Ivybridge

The Rushing River

The rushing river was
Speeding over the rocks,
Eroding and raging,
Smashing branches,
On its way,
Flowing and foaming,
Crashing against the bank.

Charlie Tapp (8)
Manor Primary School, Ivybridge

My River

Oozing and dripping,
Slowly pushing,
Splashing down the river.

Rippling and gushing,
Eating and eroding,
My river finally meets the sea.

Nicole Grech-Cini (8)
Manor Primary School, Ivybridge

The River Erme

Turning and twisting
Falling and flowing
Swirling and slipping
Slurping and splashing
Whirling and whooshing.

Ella Beardsley (7)
Manor Primary School, Ivybridge

River Erme Poem

Chattering
Clattering over
The rocks and stones
Splashing and
Sploshing
Down
Down
Down
To the sea.

Hayley Dennis (8)
Manor Primary School, Ivybridge

A River Poem

A waterfall dripping onto the ground
Falling and falling
A waterfall
The waterfall
The river
The water we have
The river we need
My river.

Kyah-Nicole Evans (8)
Manor Primary School, Ivybridge

The River Dart

R ough River Dart.
I went on a boat,
V ery deep was the River Dart,
E roding, moving, running and falling,
R iver Dart ran to the sea.

James Stirk (8)
Manor Primary School, Ivybridge

The River Erme

Falling down the waterfall,
Foaming around the large rocks.
Plunging into the water,
Pushing around furiously.

Crashing into the rocks,
Cutting into the stones.
Splashing into the pool,
Slurping down the river.

Leaping out of the water,
Swirling around and around.
Slipping over the rocks,
Sliding around and down.
Dripping into the water,
Dropping down into the pool.
Whooshing while whirling.

Cara Alcock (7)
Manor Primary School, Ivybridge

The River

Falling down the waterfall,
As the lily pads go past.
Rushing water running past,
As the fish swim furiously.
Going through the back
As it leaps in and out of the water
Eating at the rocks.
The rocks go past as the river comes furiously,
It rushes past,
Splashing and sploshing,
Washing the stones away.
It's rushing over the rocks,
Diving down deep as the river goes past.
It is so cold.

Freya Taylor (7)
Manor Primary School, Ivybridge

A River Poem

Crashing river's like a bomb explosion
And a splash of a firework
Going nine feet high.
Wrinkling river like elephant skin.
Rocky river as if it was alive.
Sparkly brown like mini stars underwater
Getting very, very tired and droopy
Once awake, now asleep.

Nathanael Marklew (8)
Manor Primary School, Ivybridge

The River

See-through water,
Twisting and shooting,
Bubbling and cutting,
Rushing and falling.
The water is splashing,
The water is oozing,
Flying waves,
Crashing against the rocks.
Salt water mixing with fresh.

Connor Chilcott & Jacob Horgan (8)
Manor Primary School, Ivybridge

The Rapids

Crashing, splashing
And leaping up and down
Thundering just like lightning
Bumping up and down
And side to side.

Jacob Antony Meads (8)
Manor Primary School, Ivybridge

The River

The river
   was
      twist
       i
         n
           g
             and
    r
      u
        n
          n
           i
             n
               g
               and
                 r
                   u
                     s
                       h
                         i
                           n
                             g
                         and
                    flowing
                 and
              rippling
                   over the rocks.

Michael Beddard (7)
Manor Primary School, Ivybridge

The Waterfall

The waterfall is falling
Mashing rocks by its side.
Crashing against the water down at the bottom
And after a while the water goes calm.

Benjamin Timothy Douglass (8)
Manor Primary School, Ivybridge

The River Deep

The rushing river
Was speeding
Over the rocks
Eroding and raging
Smashing branches
On its way.

Hollie Manlow (8)
Manor Primary School, Ivybridge

The River

Falling and foaming,
Eating and eroding,
Rushing and crashing and cutting,
Falling and thundering,
Rippling and reflecting,
Falling and crashing,
Flicking and flying.

Jay Gloyn (8)
Manor Primary School, Ivybridge

Water

The river swirls
The river whirls
Into the grey, sharp rocks
You run and run and reflect the sun
You flow and flow
Until you go
Into the big blue sea.

Amy Flower (8)
Manor Primary School, Ivybridge

The Brimming Sea

I rise and brim,
I fall and spray,
I go as far
As men can say.
I come and go,
I always flow,
I swirl and curl,
I splish and splash.
I whoosh and whirl,
I sometimes swirl,
Creating a sparkling whirlpool.

Barnaby Shaw (8)
Manor Primary School, Ivybridge

Water Poem

Swirling and twirling
Stony scatter
Whooshing and swooshing
Bonybridge water scatter
Swishing and swoshing
Crashing and splashing
Flowing and slowing.

Phoebe Phillips (7)
Manor Primary School, Ivybridge

The River

The water was
Twisting and turning
Running and rushing
Flowing and raging
Over the rocks.

Oliver Brandon (7)
Manor Primary School, Ivybridge

The Life Of A Waterfall

The river is almost asleep
Flowing and gliding
Then suddenly it's awake
Falling, falling
Leaping over rocks
Smashing and bashing
It realises it is in a waterfall
It sees the end of the waterfall
Down, down
Crash!
It hits the end
And starts falling asleep again
Flowing, flowing
Then out it bubbles
Into the waves
Feeling the salt.

Amy Gibson (9)
Manor Primary School, Ivybridge

The Crashing Waterfall

The waterfall is chattering
Over stony ways
I fall over
Bumpy ways
I will go as far
As men can say
I will rise
And I will sink
I will twirl
And whirl
I will churn.

Scott Ham (9)
Manor Primary School, Ivybridge

The Waterfall

Crashing, splashing
Bashing, smashing
Dipping, dodging
Steeping, popping
Caverning, ducking
Growing, leaping
Twisting, winding
Once asleep, now awake!

James Scott Ogle (8)
Manor Primary School, Ivybridge

Beautiful Waterfall

The splashing river leaps over the rock
Crashing into the boulders.
The wind blows the water
So the water wrinkles
And starts to move
Zooming past the rock
Falling and bubbling down.

Amber Bartlett (8)
Manor Primary School, Ivybridge

A River Poem

Slipping and sliding
Splashing and splishing
Speedy and fast
Rough and tough
Racing and rushing
Twisting and turning
Smashing and crashing.

Chloe Ellen Fancett (7)
Manor Primary School, Ivybridge

The River Poem

Splashing and leaping and sliding
Crashing and smashing and zooming
And rippling and slipping
Along the rocky water
Raining and thundering
And crashing and windswept
Twisting to the sea
The river meets the mouth.

Karina Jones (7)
Manor Primary School, Ivybridge

A River Poem

A wavy river moves calmly along the riverbank.
It's vibrating in my hand.
I can hear bubbling in the middle of the river
When I close my eyes and lie down.
It is a clanging noise.
My river.

Alice May Handley (8)
Manor Primary School, Ivybridge

The Waterfall

Crashing, bashing
Smashing, popping
Dipping, leaping
Crushing, jumping
Bumping, hitting
Thundering sounds.

Blake Alexander Chapman (8)
Manor Primary School, Ivybridge

The River Poem

Thundering and swishing.
Breaking and smashing.
Foaming and crashing.
Splashing and leaping.
Rapidly twisting.
Winter cold.
Hard and strong
And zooming.

Nathan Faulkner (8)
Manor Primary School, Ivybridge

A River Poem

Rapid, fast
Rushing speedily
Wavy river
Splashing rocks
Thundering past
Loud crashing!

Tristan Read (7)
Manor Primary School, Ivybridge

A Rapid Poem

Rushing down the slippery river
And leaping over the edges
And going over the rocks
And roughly going over the crashing boulders
And down the stream.

Brendan James Rosier (7)
Manor Primary School, Ivybridge

The Waterfall Poem

Fastly going down the waterfall
Very fast water going down the waterfall
Speedy, rough waterfall splashing down
Thundering down the rapids
Creeping down the riverbank
It is very rough and very noisy
Rushing down to the mouth
Rushing, crashing and splashing against the rocks.

Kieran J Brown (7)
Manor Primary School, Ivybridge

A River Poem

The river smashes and crashes over the rocks.
The stripes have fights and pop up at the bottom.
The water moves quickly when it hits the bottom.
It sounds like an explosion.
The water is wrinkly and moves swiftly.
The big, splashing waterfall
Crashes over the thunderball boulders.
The speedy river bombs down on the waterfall.

Matt Buckley (8)
Manor Primary School, Ivybridge

A River Poem

The water is twisting
And turning and whirling
Speeds over the rocks
Quickly splashing on the rushing rocks.

Chloë Williams (8)
Manor Primary School, Ivybridge

The Tree

On a cool day in spring
The tree
Thinks he'll make some pink blossom
And pleads the buds to open
And rests his black bark
On his thin skin

On a scorching day in summer
The tree
Looks at the people
Resting under him
He sweats under the roasting sun
And smiles at the burning sun

On a multicoloured day in autumn
The tree wakes up with no green leaves
He's about to cry when
He sees he has red leaves instead

On an icy day in winter
The tree
Weeps for his leaves
Now covered in snow
He thinks,
When will spring come?

Jonathon Pink (8)
St Joseph's Catholic Primary School, Devonport

Harvest

H arvest is here.
A mber apples and golden corn.
R ipe crops ready to eat.
V ines of grapes ready to make wine.
E veryone is looking forward to harvest.
S eeds have grown into crops.
T he harvest means everything and we thank God for it.

Liam Ferguson (10)
St Joseph's Catholic Primary School, Devonport

Candle

There's a candle,
Shining bright,
On this cold,
Winter's night.

Owls do hoot,
Yet all is still,
Except the cat,
On the window sill.

The sparrow's young,
Have flown the nest.
The robin died,
We miss his red breast.

But still the candle,
Flickers on,
And won't go out,
Till early morn.

Rebecca Pink (9)
St Joseph's Catholic Primary School, Devonport

The Door

(Inspired by 'The Door' by Miroslav Holub)

Go and open the door
Maybe there will be a tank
Of hungry sharks or a fat cat
And a small dog fighting with each other.

Go and open the door
Maybe there will be a big eye watching me
Or a cool band playing a rock song.

Go and open the door
Maybe there will be a city made of milk chocolate
Or the talented army surrounding the house.

Cohen Officer (8)
St Joseph's Catholic Primary School, Devonport

The Door

(Inspired by 'The Door' by Miroslav Holub)

Go and open the door
Maybe there is a big eye
Or a dog sitting on a log
Or maybe a little man.

Go and open the door
Maybe there is a secret garden
Or a pink, crystal palace
Maybe a princess.

Go and open the door
Maybe Action Man's there
Or a bright light
Even Barbie might be there.

Open the door
There must be a draught.

Lauren Winchester (8)
St Joseph's Catholic Primary School, Devonport

Harvest

The combine harvester passes by
Glistening dewdrops on the barley and rye
The leafy streets
The field of wheat
The ripe fruit
In the apple tree

The busy workers in the mill
The bread is baked but still
The wheat is being collected in
The golden stalks

God is helping us to grow the harvest
He is helping us to collect it in
Can He taste the lovely harvest?
All His crops collected in.

Emily Futcher (9)
St Joseph's Catholic Primary School, Devonport

The Weird But Wonderful Family

There was a young boy
That was full of joy
And then one day
He ran away
His mother and father were very sad
And said, 'How could he be so bad?'
He came back with a smile on his face
But someone was sitting in his place
He said to his dad, 'Who is this?'
'This is your new brother Kris.'

'I don't want a new brother,'
He said to his mother.
'He is very nice,' she said,
'But he's sleeping in my bed.'
'Oh dear, oh dear,
We'll kick him out of here.'
And then he cheered
But he felt really weird
He went to sleep in his bed
But then he saw it was red.

'Mother, my bed is red.'
'Then you'll have to sleep in my bed.'
'But I want to sleep in the spare room.'
'No, it smells like a mouldy spoon.'
'Oh dear, oh dear, what am I to do?'
'You can sleep with your brother
But he keeps going *moo*!'
'Oh Dad, oh Dad.'
'Son, why are you looking so sad?'
'My bed is red, the spare room smells like a mouldy spoon
And my brother keeps going *moo*!'
'Oh dear, what is the family going to do?'

Maeve Dennehy (9)
St Joseph's Catholic Primary School, Devonport

The Door

(Inspired by 'The Door' by Miroslav Holub)

Go and open the door
Maybe there's a secret garden
Or a fiery dragon.

Go and open the door
Maybe there's a fiery dragon
Or there could be an eye.

Go and open the door
There could be a monster
Or a scary tiger.
OK, but there's a draught.

Lucy Fowell (7)
St Joseph's Catholic Primary School, Devonport

Old Oliver MacDonald

Oliver MacDonald is very, very old
Eighty-seven years at least,
He's lived in the city all of his life
In a cottage out to the east.

This city he lives in was once a small town
Surrounded by fields so green,
From this town MacDonald remembers each day
His childhood that only he's seen.

Day after day he visits the park
Full of broken carts and rides,
And there Oliver sees a vision of himself
So young and so happy on the slides.

He sits there silently on the broken bench
Like a ghost that never blinks,
Memories floating in the deserted park
He stays there all day and thinks.

Matthew Luke (11)
Stowford Primary School, Ivybridge

Old John Road

Poor John Road is very, very old,
Eighty-five years or more,
He's lived in Plymouth all his life,
In his flat on the very top floor.

With multiple fillings, his teeth are black,
And his joints are awfully creaky,
His greasy hair is white and slick,
His shoes are black and squeaky.

Day after day he makes his way,
To the park where he used to play,
He sits on the bench, familiar and old,
And remembers his childhood days.

'My old friend Joe, best pals we were,
Running and kicking a ball,
Sailing our boats along the stream,
To the rickety bridge by the wall.

That old stone wall could tell its tale,
Of our endless army games,
From a gun post to a castle it was,
Which we said went up in flames.

Little did we know back then,
That this would all come true,
The war broke out so suddenly,
We realised we hadn't a clue.

My mother was forced to go to work,
Father went out to war,
Joe was asked to evacuate,
We played together no more.'

Keziah Stephenson (10)
Stowford Primary School, Ivybridge

Shadow Acrostic Poem

S hadows are dark.
H uge shadows, small shadows.
A shadow can be faint.
D ark shadows can be big.
O ur shadows copy us.
W hen the sun is out you get a shadow.
S unny days give you a shadow.

Jordan Kane (8)
Stuart Road Primary School, Stoke

Shadows

S howing in the light
H anging around us
A peing our movements
D isappearing in the dark
O ut in the sunshine again
W here we have fun
S hadow and me.

Sunni Elder (7)
Stuart Road Primary School, Stoke

Shadows Are Formed

S hadows are formed when light hits an object
H igh and low, it depends where shadows and sunlight are
A ny type of shadow, high and small, the shadow is still there
D ying sunlight goes and night arrives
O f all the shadows every one sticks to you unless it is dark
W inter sunlight is darker and shadows are blacker.

Eleanor Aquitaine (7)
Stuart Road Primary School, Stoke

Shadows

S un up high
H ere it comes
A bove me now
D own on the ground
O ut my shadow pops
W atch it grow, my
S hadow.

Miluse Hokyova & Ashley Russell (7)
Stuart Road Primary School, Stoke

Shadows

S hadows and sunlight
H uge shadows
A mazing shadows
D ark little shadows
O range shadows
W hipping big shadows
S hadows.

Megan Rowland (7)
Stuart Road Primary School, Stoke

Shadows

S mall and big
H igh and low
A ll shadows need light
D id you know
O nly you can't stand on your shadow
W hy don't you give it a go?
S ee how many are out today.

Harry Hayward (8)
Stuart Road Primary School, Stoke

Shadows

S hadows are formed when light shines on an object but cannot pass through it.

H azy shadows, haunting shadows are in old and haunted houses.

A t night-time shadows are sometimes seen.

D aylight forms shadows.

O utside, inside, there's always a shadow.

W arm, sunny, summer days are when shadows come out.

S hadows are black or grey.

Eleanor Cheesman (7)
Stuart Road Primary School, Stoke

Shadows

S hadows are dark.

H ere comes my shadow.

A long comes a dog shadow.

D own the sun goes.

O n the street you see shadows.

W alking on the street with my shadow.

S hadows are grey.

Ritchie Reynolds (7)
Stuart Road Primary School, Stoke

Shadows

S un makes shadows

H ere and there

A ll around

D own and up

O ver and under

W herever you look

S hadows are fun.

Josh Snow (7)
Stuart Road Primary School, Stoke

Shadows

S hadows are blacked by the light
H iding from the shapes
A nd the patterns
D on't be scared my mum says
O wls making noises in the background
W aiting for the night to end
S hapes, sounds all around, sleeping is not easy.

Lewis Withers (7)
Stuart Road Primary School, Stoke

Shadows

S hadows are fun
H uge shadows, small shadows
A nd very dark shadows
D ay shadows, night shadows
O utdoor shadows, indoor shadows
W alls have shadows too
S hadows of me, shadows of you.

Danielle Hines (8)
Stuart Road Primary School, Stoke

Shadows

S hadows are big, shadows are small
H ave you ever seen your shadow at all?
A ll shadows are all
D ifferent shapes and sizes
O utside, inside, there's always one there!
W e all have shadows
S o look out for your shadow.

Taylor Olver (8)
Stuart Road Primary School, Stoke

Shadows

S hadows are formed from the sun
H uge shadows
A nd small shadows
D etail on shadows - there isn't any
O nly your shadow will look like you
W here the sun is the shadow is formed differently
S o the sun is the main light source.

Kathryn Wardle (8)
Stuart Road Primary School, Stoke

Shadows

S hadows are formed when the sun shines
H uge shadows, small shadows
A ttached to my feet is my friend
D ark man dancing wherever I go
O n walls, over bushes, following me
W hen I stop, he stops, always with me
S o long as the sun keeps shining.

Tobias Moore (7)
Stuart Road Primary School, Stoke

Shadows

S hadows can be different shapes and sizes.
H ow many shape shadows?
A ny shape shadows.
D ifferent shaped shadows everywhere.
O pen your mouth - your shadow doesn't change.
W hich shadow is the best? I don't really know.
S hadows are fantastic.

Rebecca Welbourn (8)
Stuart Road Primary School, Stoke

What Does Autumn Mean To Me?

Crusty bread and dripping butter,
Hot soup on the boil,
Treacle tart and creamy custard,
Potatoes wrapped in foil.

Apple and raspberry crumble,
Hot scones with jam,
Strawberries and cream,
'Roasted chestnuts are ready, Sam.'

'Wipe your feet!' mums say -
Big, furry boots being dragged on,
Mist as thick as cloud -
Where has the sun gone?

Acorn cups being collected in baskets,
Fur cone girls being made,
Crispy leaves and bare, brown trees,
Leaves being shovelled with spades.

Josana Hayles (8)
Stuart Road Primary School, Stoke

What Does Autumn Mean To Me?

Sunsets sinking down, in the night sunsets die.
Fruits taste beautiful when you pick them off the trees.
Air blows windy and frosty in the mornings.
Trees grown bare and brown.
Leaves colourful, gorgeous, laying on the ground
And hanging from the trees.
Autumn is the best time of the year.

Shannon Nation (8)
Stuart Road Primary School, Stoke

A Walk In Autumn

Big, bold boots.
Mud is churning.
The owl hoots.
Fire is burning.

Apple crumble
And blackberry pie.
As a squirrel
Scampers by.

Chestnuts gleaming.
Leaves are brown and crispy.
Birds are leaving.
It is very misty.

Crunch the leaves go
Like an alligator.
There's nearly snow.
See you later.

Olivia Evenden (8)
Stuart Road Primary School, Stoke

Autumn Strikes Back

The bags are scattering,
The hedgehogs are marching,
As if they were scorching.
The dark woods,
The whistling winds,
But trees are strong,
The trees are waving,
The rolling bags of leaves,
The howling owls,
The dark wood
And the winter is approaching.

Vasily Babichev (8)
Stuart Road Primary School, Stoke

Autumn Leaves

Leaves crispy.
Brown leaves.
Bags full of leaves.
All crunchy and sweet like apples in tinfoil.
All nice and warm and hot like roast potatoes.

Dylan George (8)
Stuart Road Primary School, Stoke

Autumn Time

Conkers are as shiny as a car.
The mist is as damp as a water slide.
Blackberries are as sweet as chocolate.
Wind is as cold as ice cream.
Trees are as bare as a pencil.

Oliver Newton (8)
Stuart Road Primary School, Stoke

Autumn

Leaves are as golden as a golden statue.
Paths are as slippy as slime.
Dogs are as cold as ice cream.
Conkers are as shiny as cars.
People are wrapped up like Eskimos.
People have their fires on as hot as the sun.
People with extra hot chocolate.

Daniel Collier (8)
Stuart Road Primary School, Stoke

This Is Autumn

Hopping rabbits,
Skipping squirrels,
Fluttering robins,
Pecking blackbirds,
Rosy-red berries,
Sweet apples,
Golden chestnuts,
Purple blackberries, misty fog,
Hot scones,
Blazing porridge,
Shining blackberries,
Misty fog,
Spiky conkers,
Woolly scarf,
Frosted hail falling down,
Warm fires,
Whistling wind,
Winter is approaching!

Carmen Kirkby (8)
Stuart Road Primary School, Stoke

Autumn Time

What does autumn mean to me?
Twirling, spinning, swirling leaves
Round, solid conkers falling down.
Bitter cold wind blowing the leaves.
Damp, freezing rain to wet the grass.
Blackberries, purple as violets.
Thick, bare trees, brown like conkers
Thick, bare, brown branches.

George May (8)
Stuart Road Primary School, Stoke

What Do You Think Of Autumn?

Roasted chestnuts by the fire,
Crumbling leaves when you walk,
Crusty bread in the morning is lovely to eat.
The cold, wailing wind is very cold.
Strawberries and cream with scones.
Squirrels collecting acorns ready for hibernation.
Mist as thick as cloud.

Teddy Thompson (8)
Stuart Road Primary School, Stoke

Autumn

Crispy, brown leaves.
All the leaves have fallen off the trees.
Cold, whistling wind like cold and windy days.
Animals storing food.
Picking blackberries, purple, black and red berries.
Dark and misty days like smoke in the air.
Rain tipping down like cold rain tipping on my hair.

Lauren Stewart (8)
Stuart Road Primary School, Stoke

Autumn Is Cold

Autumn is freezing cold.
The leaves are rustling.
The trees are creaking.
The people are cold and the animals are cold.

Nathan Kerr (7)
Stuart Road Primary School, Stoke

Autumn

Leaves rustle in the wind
Like a lion growling.
Trees sway in the breeze
As the wind blows.
Wind whistling,
Wind whistles
Like a bird.
Bumpy branches get in my way
Like tigers' claws.

Jack Robinson (8)
Stuart Road Primary School, Stoke

Mist And Rain

Crackling leaves
Juicy blackberries
Grey, spooky mist
Conkers splitting into quarters
The broken branches
The red, fiery leaves
The plants are dying
The wind is whistling around my ears.

Thomas Bellamy (8)
Stuart Road Primary School, Stoke

Autumn

Blackberries as purple as sunset.
Misty days are grey and black.
Flower blossoms falling.
Hard, heavy rain.

Kiera Symons (8)
Stuart Road Primary School, Stoke

Autumn Is Here

What does autumn mean to me?

Leaves are very, very brown and crispy!
Hot chocolate being drunk
Running down their throats!
When you go out
You can feel the very, very breezy wind
Smoke coming out of chimneys really fast
Everybody is wearing a woolly coat
When it becomes dawn the sky becomes purple
That's the beautiful sunset
In the morning you can see the mist through the window.

Aimee Boniface (8)
Stuart Road Primary School, Stoke

Autumn Days

Conkers are falling like meteors
Wind is coming like a hurricane
Rain falls like hailstones
Smoke is coming out of chimneys like bonfires in the cold breeze
Soup is cooking like a jacuzzi bubbling on the cooker
Cocoa is going down people's throats
Like a water slide in the summer sun.

Jack Pullinger-Ham (8)
Stuart Road Primary School, Stoke

Autumn

Leaves float down from trees.
Flowers are dying.
Birds flying away now.
Blackberries are ready to eat.
Mist as thick as wind.

Hannah Sansom (8)
Stuart Road Primary School, Stoke

Dartmoor In Autumn

Mist is thick.
Leaves like fire.
Nights are longer.
Days are shorter.
Evenings are cooler.
Fires are lit.
Blackberries big, fat and juicy.
Squirrels with acorns in their mouths.
Flowers turn brown and fall.
Raindrops fall off trees.
In autumn I wear a coat.
Mums say, 'Crumble's hot.'
Warm, crusty bread.
Cream on my scones.

Millie Brown (8)
Stuart Road Primary School, Stoke

Autumn Is Here!

Leaves - crispy brown, rustling sounds
Leaves - big block of leaves
Sheds - of tools
Trees - green mould coming off branches
Bare branches with no leaves
Weather - weather is cold
Flower - blossom coming off
Misty days are grey and black
Rain - rain is heavy
Squirrels are stuffing chestnuts
So they can get fat to keep warm in the autumn.

Chantel Jenkins (8)
Stuart Road Primary School, Stoke

Do You Like Autumn?

Leaves, dirty and cold and damp.
Damp as ice coming off.
Blackberries are lovely and warm as a radiator outside.
Wind blowing like an umbrella in the sky.
Flowers, petals coming off.
Flowers dying in the cold.
Animals in their homes cuddling together
As cuddly as a banana being eaten.
Chestnuts shining and warm.
Outside on the floor they are damp.
Garden food, carrots come out of the ground
Being washed in the freezing cold water.
The water is as cold as a bird in the nest.
Chocolate frozen as a choc ice.
Flies buzzing around the place
And eating honey for themselves,
Flies have got as many as a honey bear.

Ellie Jackson (9)
Stuart Road Primary School, Stoke

Autumn Is Here!

Golden-brown leaves are crisp.
Trees are bare with yellow branches.
Bags full of leaves in the shed.
Bubbles in the hot bath.
Mums cooking scones in the oven.
Blackberries shining in the sun.
Misty in the morning.
Candlelight next to my bed.
Animals hiding their food for winter.

Hannah Atkins (8)
Stuart Road Primary School, Stoke

Autumn

Leaves are crispy and light.
Conkers are hard and fall heavily.
The sun is out but it's a cold breeze.
Rain is falling, *drop, drop, drop* from muddy clouds.
Mist is coming now so get in shelter, it's going to rain.
Wind is cold but the sun is out.
Chestnuts are falling down, one landed on my foot - *awww!*

Adam Olver (8)
Stuart Road Primary School, Stoke

The Evil Candle

A box-shaped building in the middle of a field,
There's a candle on the floor.
He sits thinking of ruling the world
Until someone breaks his peace.

A boy stumbles into the building
He starts to explore the room
And finally the candle asks,
'Who dares break my peace?'

The boy says, 'Who goes there?'
As he shivers in his shoes.
The candle answers, 'Me.
Why did you break my peace?'

He asks the candle,
'What's this building doing here?'
The candle answers, 'It's the box of evil.
You still haven't answered why you broke my peace.'

The boy runs out the room
He runs and runs and runs,
The candle sits waiting for another stranger,
To break his peace.

Amy Marshall (10)
Tidcombe Primary School, Tiverton

Hurricane Katrina Strikes

She travelled from sea to a city nearby spiralling round and round
Impossible to stop
She chased thousands of people into houses and domes
Ruining houses, homes and innocent people.

She flew like a bird coming down and down
Picking things up and dropping them on the floor
Scaring people away from their home and country.

A huge wave climbed over the levee
Fierce winds breaking the weak wall
Letting the water out, causing dreadful flooding
People shivering as they look out their smashed windows.

The horrid hurricane has stopped
And the scary storm has frozen
They don't have anything, not even a home
Just large monstrous flood water.

Caragh Matthews (10)
Tidcombe Primary School, Tiverton

Before, Then And After

Gushing winds torpedoing high,
Soaking warm moisture as she goes by,
It's coming here, trudging west,
She's trekking along and over our land,
Like a lion ripping its prey apart.

New Orleans lies deep in devastation,
Everything must start again,
Levies torn in half like a heart,
People lying dead in streets,
Families demolished apart from each other.

She won her battle and killed many,
Sorrow lies deep in New Orleans,
Buildings wrecked, homes are most flooded,
This is a disaster and another one begins.

Louise Dunn (10)
Tidcombe Primary School, Tiverton

Katrina

She is crouching on top of the sea,
Coming to show everyone
What she can be.
She comes along like a cloud.

The deadly wind comes shockingly
Past like a lightning bolt,
That no one can stop,
She makes her move in the dark night's light.

Cars are flying down the street,
Ready for Katrina to beat
Eating it like a piece of meat,
But she's got no plate, she's just a state.

Dominic Mottram (10)
Tidcombe Primary School, Tiverton

Candlelight

Here is the candle as lonely as it seems
You can see my flickering red beams
Although my candlelight has gone
Can you light me again?
Alas I am reborn again
Oh it's you little girl, hey I am trying to talk to you
I am never going to forget you
In this lonely small world
In this lonely small room.
I am never going to forget you.

Madeleine Ell (10)
Tidcombe Primary School, Tiverton

The Candlelight Horse

A candle waited in a stable,
All alone.
Around it was dark, soothing air
It cried out for someone, anyone.

A light flicked on,
Then the sound of feet,
'Are they coming to me?'
The sound went past.

They came back,
The latch slid across,
The feet came in,
And paused.

Over to the candle
They went,
Flick
Then *flare*.

A horse stood there,
Gleaming in the moonlight,
It was the . . .
Candlelight horse.

The feet got on,
And they flew through the air,
He started to melt,
It was the end.

The feet got off
And left him,
Just standing there,
Crying, dying but in peace.

Megan Pharaoh (10)
Tidcombe Primary School, Tiverton

Candle Poem

In a land dark and cold
Where mysterious sounds echo and fade
By the sound of lightning
There was a candle
Standing peacefully.

This candle was gold
Resting and waiting
For a new life
A life of fun and thought
Then something was moving
In the scary dark room.

It reached out for him
Picked him up by his base
Now the candle was shivering in fear
Suddenly he was lit
His dreams fulfilled
All around the room light.

The room was beautiful
Blue carpet, blue walls
It was like the sky
In the corner people
Three happy people
Crying in happiness.

The candle dancing in joy
His smile was like a thousand suns
The twinkle in his eyes
Saying more than words could ever say
Alone in the dark no more
Happy forever.

Joseph Taylor (10)
Tidcombe Primary School, Tiverton

Hurricane Madness

Bubbling, fast, treacherous, scary,
A terrible storm about to be born.
She lifts her head and sees her prey,
She will show no mercy.

Twisting, turning, picking up speed
She is nearly there
She is going to unleash her power,
The worst storm ever.

She picks up a roof
And crumbles it to dust,
Like a child throwing dirt rocks,
The people inside try to flee!
She cries, 'There is no escaping from me.'

Moving along, the rain is pouring
The rivers have burst their banks,
The thunder is roaring,
The lightning comes down like a sword
The worst storm has come.

Cars are flowing down the street
She is angry, raging and really deadly,
The houses are mangled
The people are dead
She is on her way once more.

She hurts, she destroyed all these lives
Pleased with her doings,
She leaves the city
With the downhearted people watching her go.

Amber Gannon (11)
Tidcombe Primary School, Tiverton

The Daydreamer

There was a candle in a dark gloomy church,
With some candles that were lit at the end of the room from a service.
The candle was daydreaming about the world outside,
Dreaming of the world above, wondering what he was meant to be

When one of the candles jumped up from the end of the room,
And came slowly bobbing towards him,
The candle turned and waved and smiled as it stopped beside him,
And looked behind him as three more candles came

And they lit the candle with a bright yellow flame,
And the candle felt love and life again,
And the candle looked up at the people who saved him,
And smiled at them in delight, with big red eyes

And the candle jumped up and flew round the church,
The others not far behind, he closed his eyes,
And fell to the ground, he tried to stand up,
But his legs had gone, and so had his arms.

They had shrunk his clothes in the wash,
The three candles had gone and now there was only one.
He blew out the candle and turned and was gone,
And slowly the little candle sat and cried, wanting to die!

Lauren Pincombe (11)
Tidcombe Primary School, Tiverton

On The Way To Texas

On the way to Texas
Calls hurricane Rita
Going over the jungle
Knocks down a herd of trees.

In a bad mood
On a mission
Can't stop now
Got to destroy Texas.

Spinning round and round
Following a cloud,
Can't catch it up
Going too fast.

Nearly there
Ten more miles
Can't stop now
On a mission.

Swish, swish, swish
This is fun, fun, fun
Destroying Texas
Now, now, now.

Dylan Penberthy (10)
Tidcombe Primary School, Tiverton

The Candle With Eyes

I can see the colour around me,
A red pillow,
A pink baby that will never grow up,
And a broken china cup.

I can feel the coldness
As it shivers down my wax
It feels like snow
It makes me think of a winter show.

I can see the stuffed teddies
As they cuddle into the bed,
They are trying to wave hi
And that's what I see with my eyes.

Bethany Morrish (10)
Tidcombe Primary School, Tiverton

Hurricane Poem

Hurricane swirl like a gymnast
Doing a spinning flip
Landing hard on the ground
Twirling round and round.

Can't stop now, gotta keep going
Ripping up my quiet view
Becoming devastating
Leaving no stone unturned.

A diver diving off a board
Into the water
Like spinning tops of doom
Using its energy.

Robbie Pengelly (11)
Tidcombe Primary School, Tiverton

The Candle Song

She's risen up
From an unwoken sleep
And is surrounded by
A school of lights.

She flicks and floats
Dancing and gliding,
Till someone plucks her up,
And cradles her home.

She's top of the world
And flying and leaping,
She's getting smaller,
But still burns on.

Leaning over to one side
And she's melting,
But still she is,
Dancing around.

She's descending now,
The end of her journey,
Flames licking round her,
Going out with a puff.

Sarah Taylor (10)
Tidcombe Primary School, Tiverton

The Dancing Candle

The candle was asleep in the dining room,
I lit her, she felt happy
She danced and glided while she shivered in the cold breeze,
I saw her wave at me, I felt the air come to me,
I thought she wanted to say something to me,
I saw her melting, she started to cry,
She said, 'Bye,' she felt very sad like she was dying,
She started to melt, she was shrinking,
Bye-bye, I will never forget you,
The candle was never lit again.

Yasmin Huish (10)
Tidcombe Primary School, Tiverton

The Boy With The Candle

I was all alone at 10 o'clock
When suddenly the bells started ringing
When all the snow you can imagine
Came down for Christmas Eve.

Everyone came in with hands like ice
They picked up candles and lit them
To keep their hands warm and nice
Like ice melting thick and fast.

Everyone's hands were as hot as fire
I could see a boy on his own,
Looking through the bookshelves,
Wondering what he was doing.

A big cold hand picked me up
Which made me shake with horror
He moved towards the bookshelf
Oh what was he doing?

I could see the dusty books
As I got close he suddenly stopped
He put his hand out and grabbed a book
Called 'Horror of the Candle Maker'.

Elliott Howells (10)
Tidcombe Primary School, Tiverton

The Black Ballerina

The ballerina comes to life,
When someone comes with a burning flame
Near the door her partner waits to be kindled.

As they go to the centre of the room a violin begins to play,
They dance and the song comes to an end.

When the flames die down
They go to their original places
The flames go out and the room
Is quiet once again.

Josie Russell-Cox (10)
Tidcombe Primary School, Tiverton

Loving And Leaving

I can see a candle being lit
By his owner he's got a lovely flame
Long getting bigger,
But as he grows his candle body gets smaller.

His owner is crying
I can see he is trying to help,
Waving his flame and hoping for attention
But no response at all.

He tries so hard
Like a flower trying to root in winter
And a tramp looking for a house
The candle takes no more.

After all his work
He melts
And all that's left . . .
A few melted tears.

Eloise Harcombe (11)
Tidcombe Primary School, Tiverton

One Sad Night

She slipped quietly into the room,
She lit the sleeping candle,
A flame appeared and began to dance,
'Where is my partner?'

He heard a calming voice,
'Here I am,' she said,
He looked frantically for her,
'Where are you?'

He burst out in tears, shrinking more and more,
'Don't cry,' she said to him,
The crying stopped and it went silent,
'Where have you gone?'

Grace Drew (10)
Tidcombe Primary School, Tiverton

A Candlelight, Shining So Bright

There once was a candle
All alone and sad
He was sad
Because he was not lit.

He was still sad
Until a family came along
He knew there was hope
He wished that they'd come to him.

They went outside to see a beloved family member
Would they come to him?
There's a hope.

The family went into the church
Walking his way
They got a match and lit the match to light him.

The church lit up,
It was like the family member was coming to life once more,
But it was the candle coming to life.

Nathanael Kidner (10)
Tidcombe Primary School, Tiverton

Saying Goodbye

I stand here day and night
Being reborn over and over again.
I explore different things every day.
I slowly melt, feeling like I want to speak,
I feel almost lonely,
Nobody knows I'm here.

I wave, but nothing happens,
I shrink as I watch the people walking towards me.
I know I'm going again
I don't want to leave but I can't do anything.
Then I'm put out again.

Gemma Mogford (10)
Tidcombe Primary School, Tiverton

The Special Evening

She strolls into the room
And strikes a match
The smell of summer fruits fills the air.

She moves closer to the flames
To smell the sweet scent
She hears someone say her name
And wonders who it is.

'Who said that?' she asks in astonishment.
'It's me, the candle,' says the lonely voice.

She is quiet for a few minutes,
Then she says, 'Oh my goodness me.'

She says, 'When I was younger,
I imagined a candle was speaking
As the flame waved about
But I was only imagining it,
And I never thought
It would really happen
In real life!'

Katie Stribley (10)
Tidcombe Primary School, Tiverton

Flickering

Flickering in the moonlight
As it floats in the pond.

Floating gracefully as a swan
With fish bobbing up and down.

Tangling in the light
Tangling like a person in the morning
With knotty hair.

As they eat in the candlelight
And the moonlight
And they're blowing out the candles in the pond.

Crystal Gardiner (10)
Tidcombe Primary School, Tiverton

If I Were A Shape

If I were a shape
I'd be a circle
I'd be a hole in a bucket
I'd be a bouncing ball bouncing down a hill
I'd be a planet in the sky
If I were a circle.

If I were a cone
I'd be the turret in a princess' palace
I'd be the top of a rocket
I'd be an everlasting ice cream cone
If I were a cone.

If I were a triangle
I'd be the top of a home
I'd be the sail from a boat sailing to Spain
I'd be the hat of a princess
If I were a triangle.

If I were I star I would be . . .
Kylie Minogue.

Hannah Stagg (8)
Tregadillett Community Primary School, Launceston

If I Were A Shape . . .

I'd be a circle
I'd be a cricket pitch where
England always wins.
I'd be a clock ticking away
I'd be a warship's cannon sinking other ships
If I were a circle.

I'd be a cone
I'd be a rocket blasting to space
I'd be a T-rex's sharp tooth
Ripping flesh
I'd be a sharp sword slaying a dragon
If I were a cone.

I'd be a rectangle
I'd be a yu-gi-oh cards thrashing people
I'd be a car speeding through the air
I'd be a muddy rugby pitch slipping people up
If I were a rectangle.

But if I were a star
I'd be Andrew Flintoff.

Daniel Pike (8)
Tregadillett Community Primary School, Launceston

Cats

My cat can see
So far away.

My cat is as smooth and silky as a fur coat,
She's as loud as a yelling elephant,
Her purr sounds like a washing machine.

My cat is as fast as a sprinting cheetah
She pounces like a crazy mouse!
She even jumps like a kangaroo!

My cat's belly is bobbly and wobbly,
Her tail is so long
Fluffy and puffy as well!

After a while
She's such a sleepy puss
Zzzzz!

Joanna Turvill (9)
Tregadillett Community Primary School, Launceston

If I Were A Shape

If I were a shape
I'd be a rectangle
I'd be a table with sweets on me,
I'd be a mouth-watering chocolate bar,
I'd be the body of a spaceship,
If I were a rectangle.

If I were a square,
I'd be a robot going up into space,
I'd be a TV playing freaky movies,
I'd be a window looking outside,
If I were square.

If I were a star,
I'd be Neil Armstrong.

Hugh Harvey (8)
Tregadillett Community Primary School, Launceston

Cats

My cat can pounce like an angry tiger.
He can also bounce like an extremely bouncy ball.

My cat can stretch like an elastic band,
He also can hiss like a wild cobra attacking.

My cat jumps like a human on
A high-jumping pogo stick.

My cat is speedy like a Formula 1 car,
Racing by like the super strike of lightning.

My cat is cuddly like a huge warm bed
My cat is brave like a knight
Trying to slay a dragon.

Nathan James (8)
Tregadillett Community Primary School, Launceston

If I Were A Shape . . .

I'd be a rectangle
I'd be a tennis court
I'd be a white snowy chocolate bar
I'd be a bedtime story book
If I were a rectangle.

I'd be a circle
I'd be a bouncy ball bouncing to America
I'd be a wheel on a limousine
I'd be a muffin, warm and ready to eat
If I were a circle.

If I were a star
I'd be Britney Spears!

Lucy Hamilton (8)
Tregadillett Community Primary School, Launceston

If I Were A Shape . . .

I'd be a cone
I'd be a cone of an ice cream
I'd be a cone from a witch's hat in the shiny night
I'd be the top of a castle, high in the sky
If I were a cone.

I'd be a triangle
I'd be a roof of a house looking down at you
I'd be a cushion so I could cuddle in with you
I'd be a rubber so I could help you with your work
If I were a triangle.

I'd be a heart
I would make you nice and kind
I'd be a yummy sweet
I'd be as red as a rose
If I were a heart.

But if I were a star . . .
I would be Britney Spears.

Evie Tummon (8)
Tregadillett Community Primary School, Launceston

The Autumn Poem

What do you see?
I see the coloured leaves falling off the trees.
What do you hear?
I hear people stepping on the crunchy leaves.
What do you taste?
I taste apple crumble.
What do you smell?
I smell the smell of amber spice.
What do you feel?
I feel my feet crunching all the leaves.

Lucy Grayston (7)
Tregony Primary School, Truro

Autumn

I can see leaves all crushed on the floor
Bare, cold trees
The icy wind.

I can hear leaves being crunched on the floor
The wind whistling in the air
Leaves dropping on the floor.

I can taste yummy blackberries
Amber spice
Autumn.

I can smell fresh air
Apple crumble
Sweet toffee apples.

I can feel me crushing the cold leaves
Cold *autumn!*

Georgina Green (8)
Tregony Primary School, Truro

Untitled

What do you see?
I see a farmer harvesting the crops.
What do you hear?
I hear the wind whistling.
What do you taste?
I taste apple crumble.
What do you smell?
I smell smoke from the garden fires.
What do you see?
I see blackberries from hedges.
What do you feel?
I feel excited because of Hallowe'en.

Benjamin Humphries (7)
Tregony Primary School, Truro

Autumn Days

I see a breeze flow past me and knock the leaves to sleep
I hear fireworks when I'm in bed,
I taste apples bobbing up and down at Hallowe'en
I smell amber spice
It reminds me of autumn
I feel cosy and warm
I like autumn.

Katie Cadby (9)
Tregony Primary School, Truro

Autumn Days

I can see brightly golden leaves.
I can hear the wind rustling in the crispy leaves.
I can taste the sweet apple pie.
I can smell the smell of leaves.
I can feel the wind pushing me.

Michael Berridge (9)
Tregony Primary School, Truro

Autumn Spell

I see golden leaves piled high on the path
I hear the wind howling in the trees
I taste warm apple crumble in my mouth
I smell pancakes in the saucepan
I feel my hands so cold in my pile of leaves.

Eleanor Gulliford (7)
Tregony Primary School, Truro

Mrs Autumn

Can you feel the wind blowing calmly? I can.
Can you smell the roast? I can.
Can you feel the coldness of the water when you touch it? I can.
Did you know love keeps you warm? I do.
Did you see that fox? I did.
Can you hear the children playing? I can.
We love autumn, don't we?

Bethany Grant (8)
Tregony Primary School, Truro

Autumn Senses

I see loads of leaves
I hear the rustling of leaves
I taste roasted chestnuts
I smell a chill in the air
I feel cold.

Jasper Boden (7)
Tregony Primary School, Truro

I Smell Autumn

I see crisp leaves
I hear the cold in my ear
I taste the taste of dinner
I smell autumn leaves
I feel autumn's chill.

Harry Price (8)
Tregony Primary School, Truro

The Autumn Taste

I see mist rising from the river
I hear leaves rustling on the floor
I can taste a burning fry-up
I smell the sun rising down
I feel very chilly and I think my blood is going to freeze.

Rose Dixon (7)
Tregony Primary School, Truro

Autumn Day

I see the nice crispy frost on the leaves.
I hear banging from the people.
I taste brilliant marshmallows.
I smell lovely fireworks.
I feel the breeze.

Kai Pearce (8)
Tregony Primary School, Truro

Autumn Season

I can hear the whistling wind and the swaying trees.
Children stepping through the crispy leaves.
I can smell Mum cooking tea.
I can hear the flying birds whistling in the bare trees.
I can hear my mum drinking some warm tea and watching TV.
I can hear my brother picking up leaves.

Jasmine McMorran (9)
Tregony Primary School, Truro

Autumn's Coming

What do you see? I see people playing.
What do you hear? I hear people walking through leaves.
What do you taste? I taste steak and kidney pie.
What do you smell? I smell smelly cows.
What do you feel? I feel very sleepy.

Sophie Jackson (9)
Tregony Primary School, Truro

Autumn Days

I see leaves all over the place.
I hear people walking on the leaves.
I taste the warm, tasty lasagne.
I smell the sweets from Hallowe'en.

Joshua Griffiths (8)
Tregony Primary School, Truro

Spring

I see gold green leaves
I hear birds in the trees
I taste apples and other fruit
I smell bonfire smoke
I feel cold.

Jack Emery (9)
Tregony Primary School, Truro

Autumn Days

I smell toffee apples,
I taste the sweet toffee apples,
I see leaves falling,
I hear leaves crushing down on the frosty road.
I smell the autumn breeze.
I taste the cooked marshmallows.
I see people playing inside.
I hear people talking.

Andrew Barnes (9)
Tregony Primary School, Truro

The Autumn

I can smell bitter leaves and autumn air.
I can taste the sweet berries and toffee apples.
I can hear the whistling wind.
I can see the trees waving.
I can smell the marshmallows in hot chocolate!

Jamie Lee (9)
Tregony Primary School, Truro

Autumn

I can see birds making pretty patterns in the sky.
I can see the grey sky blocking us in.
I can hear the trees swaying in the gusty wind.
I love the taste of blackberry pie.
It shows us that autumn is coming.

Rachael O'Brien (9)
Tregony Primary School, Truro

Autumn Is Coming

I can see bare trees becoming colder and colder,
I can hear crunchy leaves crackling on the ground,
I can smell amber spice coming from the trees,
I can feel the coldness of the air and the warmness of the fireplace,
I can taste autumn coming.

Ysabelle Smith (8)
Tregony Primary School, Truro

Victorian Farmer Boy

Working on the farm,
Picking up stones,
Lasts all day,
Hurts my bones.

I have to scare away,
The birds from the crop,
If I don't
I will get the chop.

Working all day,
The months fly away,
Gets dark quicker,
The clouds are thicker.

Mucking out the pigs,
While they dig.

Collecting the eggs from the hens,
Shooing the sheep from their pens.

Milking the cow,
While master rings the bell,
Eating the veg,
While picking weeds from the hedge.

Noal Fawdry (10)
Troon Primary School, Camborne

Chimney Sweep

It's a cold and miserable damp street,
Water is running through my feet,
My socks are wet and soggy,
The sky is breezy, grey and foggy.

Arrive at the big house,
No choice but to work,
My boss pushes me forward,
With a nasty jerk.

Soot and dirt falling in my face,
My hands are shaking with fear,
Must earn money or sit in disgrace,
More chimneys to sweep far and near.

It feels like I'm filled with soot,
I'm aching head to foot,
It's a long way down to the floor,
Got to keep sweeping a little bit more.

Mylor Fawdry (10)
Troon Primary School, Camborne

Factory Workers

I am a poor little kid,
Abandoned on the streets,
Working in the dirty and grimy factories,
Getting my fingers,
Stuck in machines,
Lose my wage if I talk,
I might even get chucked out for the rest
Of the day.
I get smacked and punched,
Scabs are always peeling off,
And that's just a normal day for me.

Jake Bowles (9)
Troon Primary School, Camborne

Poor Chimney Children At Work

Slowly up the chimney I make,
My way slithering hard like a snake,
Have to go up or might get beat,
Need the money or won't be able to eat.

Cramped inside the chimney stack,
Grazes and bruises all over my back,
Like a woodlouse squeezing through,
Trying hard to hold onto my shoe.

Terrified of falling down,
Struggling to breathe with a frown,
In the chimney I get stuck,
Choked by soot and lots of muck.

Charlotte Wardley (10)
Troon Primary School, Camborne

Poor People

Working in factories,
Living in poor streets,
Children get fingers caught in machines,
Me and my freezing feet.

Factories dangerous, six in the morning,
Children in the street wearing rags,
My feet on the street,
Children and their mums and dads.

Horrible, smelly, black, small, cold chimneys.
Stop the Victorian children suffering please!

Andrew Figgins (10)
Troon Primary School, Camborne

Jobs That Children Do

I'm in the dirty mine
There's not much air,
Hardly any light.
Bad cuts that are bleeding to death,
Dust and dirt in my lungs
I can hardly breathe with fear.
Bricks falling everywhere
Worrying I might get hit.

I'm in a filthy factory
Where I spend most of my time.
I do it to get money
To feed my family.
My fingers get trapped
In the rusty machines.
I'm afraid of getting fired.

Scared of dying
The soot makes my lungs go black.
Crammed so tight,
I just can't breathe.
I want to get out and be free.

Amy Dillow (10)
Troon Primary School, Camborne

Chimney Sweep

My arms are aching,
My arms are shaking,
My bones are breaking,
My boss is timing,
My legs are climbing,
My people are calling,
The soot is falling,
Being a chimney sweep
It's very hard not to weep.

Tamara Browning (10)
Troon Primary School, Camborne

Coal Mine

Walking through the tunnel
Crouching low to the ground
Hoping I will see light again
Hoping coal will be found.

Sitting down by the trapdoor
Opening to let the coal come through
Hoping a cave-in will never happen
If it does, don't know what I'll do.

Grazes and cuts on my arms
Bruises all over my back
Candle lighting up the mine
And the coal truck track.

Not much money
Craving for food
Hate my job
Always in a bad mood.

Curtis Wherry (9)
Troon Primary School, Camborne

Trapper Down A Mine

Trapper down a mine,
Only ten years old,
Candles my only light,
Don't fall asleep or there might be an explosion,
Only see coal carts and a few other miners all day long,
Very lonely,
Cramped and closed in, uncomfortable,
Moving around causes scars and bruises,
Dark and dirty,
Unpleasant,
Afraid of rocks falling and the gas killing me.

Jacob Rail (10)
Troon Primary School, Camborne

The Farmyard Girl

Here I stand arms out wide,
Waiting for the blackbirds' call.
Here they come, all evil and black,
Their claws out wide waiting to attack.

My arms and legs are working day and night,
If I don't work all day I'll get a fright.
Walking bare-footed along the earth,
I've been working ever since my birth.

I hear my heart trembling with fear,
In the farm I see a baby deer.
On its own I know how it feels,
Left outside pulling the water wheels.

Amy Greig (9)
Troon Primary School, Camborne

Chimney Sweep

Fear of dying stuck in the chimney,
Black soot blinding me.
Breathing in dust,
Clogging up my lungs.
Stretching my body
Crying tears
Leaving lines,
On my face.
Tears at the skin
Full of scratches and scars.
Ripped clothes covered in coal.
Arms burning and stinging.

Liam Stone (10)
Troon Primary School, Camborne

I Don't Like Work

My job is a trapper,
I open and close doors to let air in,
But still I get gas in my lungs.
Bats scare me.
The air is thin,
Not enough money.
Food short,
Throat aches,
Life I hate.

James Wassell (9)
Troon Primary School, Camborne

I Am A Flower Girl

I am a flower girl dirty and black,
If I don't work, I'll get a smack,
Everything seems to be aching,
When I bend over my back is breaking.

All around me people are wearing beautiful clothes,
Water is running through my toes,
I'm cold, hungry and I've got nothing to wear,
I'm fed up of my life of despair!

Save the children!

Elena Hoskin (10)
Troon Primary School, Camborne

In The Mines

I am in the mines,
With no air at all,
We have to push the coal carts through the darkness,
Only one candle to light my way,
My feet are cut and grazed,
I hear someone crying for help,
My bones are aching,
I hope to see daylight soon.

Aaron Roskilly (9)
Troon Primary School, Camborne

The Chimney Sweep

Dusty and dark,
The chimney is scary,
I have a long tiring day,
My mum worries about me,
The small amount of money
I earn buys our bread and milk,
Soot in my eyes and up my nose,
Bruises on my arms and legs,
How I wish I could stay at home.

Josh Trescowthick (10)
Troon Primary School, Camborne

The Rainy Day

It was a dark and gloomy day,
And the rain made a pattering noise on the windowpane,
So no one could go out to play,
The kids were driving Mum and Dad insane.

Then a glimmer of hope came that day,
No not the sun, but the ice cream man coming down the lane.
The kids jumped up and asked if they may,
'Go on,' said Mum, 'if you stop being a pain!'

Out they trotted to the ice cream van,
One chose a rocket and the other a choc ice,
They headed back home, but as they ran,
They realised, the rain was quite nice.

Mark Godfrey (9)
Woodbury CE Primary School, Exeter

Untitled

The fat cat sat on the mat,
He was fat as Father Christmas,
He had ears like a tiger,
He had a tongue like a giraffe,
He had eyes like a gorilla,
He had fur like black sky,
He had whiskers like a straight ruler,
He had a tail like a snake,
He had a belly like jelly on a plate,
His nose was as wet as a cold winter day.

Josephine Jacka
Woodbury CE Primary School, Exeter

Fabulous Feline Family

In the night the jungle cats roam,
While the tame cats lounge at home.
The captured ones roar to the moon,
The mice squeak a scream of doom.

The fur of felines is like fluffy feather down,
While kittens wear fur dressing gowns.
Tigers in their stripy Sunday suit,
Panthers in black, stealing some loot.

They have retractable knives on each paw,
Sharp as a fiery dragon's claw.
By the moon they hunt at night,
Their pupils open, giving mice a fright.

Their tails bottle brush, at the sight of a dog,
They like to munch mice, voles and frogs.
Tame cats sleep on my warm bed,
Mighty jungle cats sleep in tall trees instead.

In the night the jungle cats roam,
While the tame cats lounge at home.
The captured ones roar to the moon,
The mice squeak a scream of doom.

Heidi Thiemann (10)
Woodbury CE Primary School, Exeter

The Monster

A little hairy monster,
Came crawling up to me,
He looked so sad and lonely,
I asked him for tea.
If only I had known the monster wanted me,
I'm down inside his stomach,
As his favourite recipe.

Ollie Woodley
Woodbury CE Primary School, Exeter

A Day In My Life

I wake up in the morning
7.30 on the dot
I was laid there yawning
As I thought the night was hot.

At school my tummy started to rumble
I couldn't wait for the bell to ring
For lunch I ate blackberry and apple crumble
Now I can take on anything.

I've done my homework best I can
I'm now waiting for my tea
The smell of cooking from Mum's pan
Yummy there is food for me.

Now the day is over
And it's drawing to a close
I cuddle my pet cat Clover
Now I'm ready for a doze.

James Ubank (10)
Woodbury CE Primary School, Exeter

Chills

I was lost in the deep dark woods,
Wandering through alone,
But then there came
A bunch of snoods,
Chewing on a bone.
Soon I legged it,
Down a hill
Until I saw a daffodil.
It was dying in the darkness.
As cold as a stormy gale,
It died that night in the dimness.

George Drew (10)
Woodbury CE Primary School, Exeter

From Darkness To Gold

The misty moon, the misty moon,
It carries with it terrible gloom,
The darkness, like a sheet, flows over its face,
Light to darkness . . . this is no race.

By dawn the moon has turned to gold,
Spreading its light that cannot be sold,
When dusk falls the fireball will set,
This is a creature that can never be met.

The light from the moon, a glowing globe,
The darkness covers it like a black satin robe,
Stillness and calm fills the air,
The vixen with cubs snuggled up in their lair.

Grace Ratley (10)
Woodbury CE Primary School, Exeter

The Dark Cave!

I was creeping carefully through a cave,
I could hear drips,
It was like being trapped in prison,
I could feel the darkness.

It went on and on like an everlasting tunnel,
It started to get narrower,
It felt like I was being swallowed up by the darkness,
I wanted to go home.

Suddenly I was blinded by a bright light,
As I turned a corner the ocean opened up to me like a huge mouth.
The waves were like a tongue lapping on the beach,
I'd left the darkness behind.

Katie Hester (10)
Woodbury CE Primary School, Exeter

Play Park

Down by the play park the time is fun,
For you and me and everyone,
Walking there from home,
Walking past the naughty gnome!

Wee, wee on the slide,
You can't say the little boy tried,
A commentator's standing on a stall,
While watching a game of football.

Now onto the super swings,
Flying up high, as a bird sings
Controlling a stray dog,
Where's its owner? Aah, sitting on a log!

Up and down jumping on a see-saw,
The whispering winds pick up an apple core,
Like two best friends sharing a joke,
The whispering winds pick up a can of Coke.

Down by the play park the time is fun
For you and me and everyone,
Coming back home
Walking past the naughty gnome!

Megan Pewsey
Woodbury CE Primary School, Exeter

The Sea Serpent

He sleeps in the sea for a century or two
But if you have pure beauty he will pop up, just for you.
He clears up the shipwrecks and the ripples go 2 by 2
His name is the sea serpent and he loves you.

Once a day a fisherman's child goes to play
Today he went to the sea just like you or me.
He rested by the 'mumble-ary' tree
As he stared at the sea.

And then from the misty sea
Came a figure ten times the size of you and me
It was the sea serpent raging like fire
He was going to strike but his claws didn't get higher.

The boy offered the serpent a lot of fish
Upon a beautiful golden dish
But then he made a desperate wish
That he had kept the beautiful dish.

Please give back my grandfather's dish
And I will give you loads more fish
The sea serpent said please don't cry
He gave him the dish and said goodbye!

Barnaby Lovell
Woodbury CE Primary School, Exeter

The Darkness

The darkness is alive . . .
Cold mist rises and kills all sense of light
The trees are talking to each other
Their low moaning voices,
Echo through the silence.
The ice is overcoming them,
Slowly their bark crumbles,
Falling onto a deathbed of broken dreams.
The soft ground is a rotting body
Calling out in silent screams,
It is more than a nightmare.
Danger passes over everything
All of the darkness becomes death.
The floor is one with the broken bodies
That litter it,
The trees are like death itself.
They sense murder,
Blood splatters the floor like eyes,
Looking up into darkness.
Deathly whispers fill the air,
Like cold wind rushing by.
Mystery overcomes the dark night,
The misty mood gives off no light,
The forest is an icy graveyard,
But there are no graves,
Just bodies.

Josh Levontine (10)
Woodbury CE Primary School, Exeter

The Highwayman

(Inspired by 'The Highwayman' by Alfred Noyes.)

Bess the landlord's daughter,
The landlord's black-eyed daughter,
Wrote a note to Highwayman
Riding-riding-riding.
The highwayman was reading:
'Go! Go! Gallop away Timmy wants to kill you.'
Timmy sent for the army-army-army.
So they came on two feet each to kill young Highwayman,
Riding-riding-riding
And to tie up Bess the landlord's daughter,
The landlord's black-eyed daughter.
As Highwayman galloped to the woods
The army tied the lassie up.
Then from the distance Highwayman heard,
Bang! The missile came right for him.
The horse galloped on as Highwayman lay in a bright
red sea of blood.
Then the horse turned back to the shocking sound
of Bess' death,
From the hellful window - the hellful window.
Timmy hadn't realised yet, as he tried to kill the horse,
The lethal gun faced his chops,
He toppled and the trigger pulled,
Death lay by the stable.
Ghosts appeared from the hellful window - the hellful window,
And the bright red sea of blood,
From the stable rose the ghost of Timmy,
Who tried to kill young Highwayman,
But *bang!* The missile went right through him.

Jozie Bannister (10)
Woodbury CE Primary School, Exeter

The Magic Box

(Based on 'Magic Box' by Kit Wright)

I will put into the box . . .
The glint of a French coin,
The crackle of some tissue paper
And a sticker from my thirtieth friend.

I will put into the box . . .
The last fluttering leaf off a tree,
The whoosh of a disc as it flies by
And the pop of a tiddlywink as it wins a game.

I will put into the box . . .
The squidge of my Blu-tack as
I clutch it in my hands,
The sparkle of some tinsel as it hangs on my tree
And the scratchy sound of my lead as it fluently
Brushes across the page.

I will put into the box . . .
My tooth as the tooth fairy takes it,
A sharpener as it makes a point on the last pencil
And the flake of a beady pencil.

My box is fashioned from
The brightest stars in the sky,
With memories in the shadows
And animals stalking their prey.
Its lid is made from
The softest dragon skin.

I shall hunt in my box
In the great rainforest of Australia
And then go home to put my boar on the spit,
To roast it for dinner.

Poppy Joyce (8)
Woodbury CE Primary School, Exeter

The Strange Dream

I stand there still, my white top flapping in the wind.
Next to me, my brother stands, black topped and quiet.
My three cousins, in front of us, bare topped and grim,
We wait, in silence, watching the starry night.

A man steps from the shadows behind
We jump, he takes my brother soundlessly.
Three others appear, out of thin air.
I stare in wonder and disbelief
As my three cousins mysteriously disappear.

Now alone, I realise how cold the night is
At last a man comes out of the shadows,
Just like the one who took my brother,
He signals, I walk
He moves into the dark
I follow him into the mist.

He turns, hands me a small object . . .
With a sudden jerk, I wake,
My brother and cousins around me sleep
I turn, there by my side
A small white marble is glittering in the moonlight.

Jocelyn Mennell (10)
Woodbury CE Primary School, Exeter